Substance ABUSE

DANTES/DSST* Study Guide

© 2016 Breely Crush Publishing, LLC

*DSST is a registered trademark of The Thomson Corporation and its affiliated companies, and does not endorse this book.

971121715143

Published by Breely Crush Publishing, LLC
10808 River Front Parkway
South Jordan, UT 84095
www.breelycrushpublishing.com

ISBN-10: 1-61433-172-3
ISBN-13: 978-1-61433-172-8

Printed and bound in the United States of America.

*DSST is a registered trademark of The Thomson Corporation and its affiliated companies, and does not endorse this book.

Table of Contents

Category	Drugs	Street Names	Medical Uses	Physical Dependence	Psychological Dependence	Tolerance	Effects	Effects of Overdose	Withdrawal Symptoms
Stimulants	Cocaine	Coke, crack	Local anesthetic	Possible	Oral- Moderate; Injected or Smoked- Very High	Possible	Increased alertness, euphoria, loss of appetite, increased pulse, insomnia	Agitation, hallucinations, convulsions, death	Depressed mood, prolonged sleep, apathy, irritability
	Amphetamines	Dexedrine, Biphetamine	Weight control, narcolepsy, hyperactivity			Yes			
	Methylphenidate	Ritalin							
	Phenmetrazine	Preludin							
	Other Stimulants	Adipex, Bacarate, Cylert							
Depressants	Chloral hydrate	Nortex	Hypnotic	Moderate	Moderate	Possible	Disorientation, difficulty speaking, walking or driving, intoxicated behavior	Cold & clammy skin, slow & shallow breathing, coma, death	Anxiety, insomnia, tremors, convulsions, death
	Barbiturates	Amytal, Butisol, Seconal	Anethestic, sedative, hypnotic	Moderate to High	Moderate to High	Yes			
	Methaqualone	Quaalude	None	High	High				
	Benzodiazepines	Atican, Dalmane, Hacion, Librium, Valium, Xanax	Anesthetic, anticonvulsant, sedative, hypnotic	Low to Moderate	Moderate to High				
	Alcohol	Large Assortment	None	Moderate	Moderate				
Cannibis	Marijuana	Pot, Grass, Weed	Used to treat pain for some Cancers	Very low	Moderate	Yes	Euphoria, increased appetite, impaired memory & attention	Fatigue, paranoia, hallucinations	Insomnia, hyperactivity
	Tetrahydrocannabinol	THC, Marinol	Glaucoma						
	Hashish	Hash	None						
Narcotics	Opium	Pentofen, Paregoric, Parepectolin	Analgesic	High	Oral – Moderate Smoked – High	Yes	Euphoria, drowsiness, nausea	Cold & clammy skin, slow & shallow breathing, coma, constricted pupils, death	Watery eyes, tremors, panic, sweating, chills, cramps, nausea
	Morphine	Morphine	Analgesic	High	Moderate				
	Codeine	Many brands	Analgesic	Moderate	Moderate				
	Heroin	Many names	Not in U.S.	High	Very High				
	Methadone	Dolophine	Analgesic, addict maintenance	High	Moderate				
Hallucinogens	LSD	Acid, many names	None	None	Low	Yes	Hallucinations, increased emotions, visual illusions	Prolonged episodes "bad trips"	Unkonwn
	Psilocybin	Mushrooms, shrooms							
	Mescaline, peyote	Mesc, cactus							
	Amphetamine variants	DOM, X, MDMA, Ecstasy		Unknown	Unknown				
	Phencyclidine	PCP Angel Dust	Veterinary Anesthetic	Very low	Moderate				

Overview

Drugs are prevalent in our society today. Stories of overdoses and arrests permeate the media. How did we get to this state? There were four pharmacological revolutions:

1. The first revolution was the introduction of vaccines that began with Pasteur. Many deadly diseases, including small pox, polio, measles, mumps, etc., have been eliminated and are well under control in developed countries. These vaccines proved to the general population that drugs are very powerful.

2. The second revolution was the introduction of antibiotics, beginning with penicillin. These drugs were first proven effective during World War II and continue to be used today. This revolution showed the general population that powerful illnesses such as pneumonia can be cured with drugs.

3. The third revolution was the creation of psychopharmachology, which began in the 1950s. This marks the creation of antipsychotic drugs which treat schizophrenia and other psychotic disorders. This revolution showed the general population that drugs can have a powerful and precise effect on our minds and emotions.

4. The fourth pharmacological revolution was the development of the oral contraceptive termed "the pill." This marks a period when drugs were not taken just by the ill or infirm but by healthy people in order to gain control over their own bodies.

Pharmacology Principles

Each drug affects each person in a different way. Why? Here are the steps that are taken to produce the desired result, for example, in introducing pain medication to a chronic arthritis sufferer.

1. A specific drug with a specific chemical structure is chosen to be used
2. The chosen drug is then measured to a certain quantity
3. Once measured, the drug is administered any number of ways (orally, injection)
4. The drug is then absorbed into the blood stream and sent to the site of the action (in this case, the joints)

How effective the drug is depends on physical characteristics of the person and how that person's body reacts with the drug. Some factors that can contribute to the effectiveness of the drug are:

- Race
- Age
- Weight
- Gender
- Drug tolerance
- Metabolism

The effect of the drug depends on how much is taken. A drug's dose is calculated based on a person's body weight. To administer the correct amount, first you must determine what the dose is equivalent to in milligrams per kilogram of body weight. Next, you need the weight of the patient in kilograms. For example, if the weight of the patient is 90kg and the dose is .10mg per kg, you would multiply the dose amount by the weight – .10kg X 90 = 9 mg of the drug.

What are the ways to administer drugs?

- Oral
- Subcutaneous (beneath the skin)
- Intramuscular (in muscle)
- Intravenous (directly into veins)
- Mucous membranes (inhalation, under the tongue, snorting or sniffing through nose)

Pharmacokinetics is the branch of pharmacology concerned with the movement of drugs within the body.

 # The Dose-Response Curve

The dose-response curve is a tool or chart that shows the effect of different doses resulting in different effects. Shown on the left is a typical dose-response curve. Basically, the higher the dose, the greater the effect.

Biphasic drug effects look like the following chart on the right. The dose response curve depends on the effect of a drug being measured. Each graph can measure a different effect. Maximal effect is the peak, or the point where the drug has the absolute most effect. Drug potency is the dose of a drug that yields the maximum effect. Metabolism is the way the body breaks down matter into simpler compounds, separating what the body needs from waste. A person's metabolism can affect the effectiveness of drugs; if the body metabolizes the drug too quickly or not quickly enough, it can effect the way the drug works.

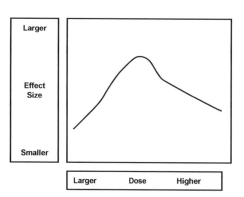
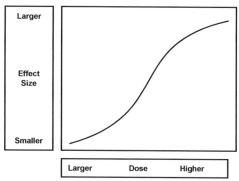

Typical Dose-response Curve   **Biphasic Drug Effects**

 # The Body's Response to Drugs

Drugs interact with human bodies causing different chemical processes to occur. These mainly take place with the nervous system. The nervous system has three main parts: the central nervous system (CNS), the somatic nervous system (which deals with sensory information), and the autonomic nervous system (which deals with involuntary bodily actions). The CNS consists of the brain and the spinal cord, thus it mostly concerns how the body reacts to drugs.

The central nervous system is made up of different molecules, the neuron being the most essential. A neuron is a cell similar to others in the body. What sets it apart is the fact that neurons communicate to each other. Each neuron has multiple dendrites, spiky structures which contain receptor sites that stick out from the neuron. Each neuron also has at least one axon, a long cylindrical structure that conducts electricity. Some of the axons in the CNS are covered in myelin, an insulating fatty substance. Between different neurons, there exists a synaptic gap. It is through this gap that different neurotransmitters, chemical messengers which are stored in tiny sacs (vesicles) within axons, cause interactions. The axons release the neurotransmitters and the dendrites have receptor sites with accept neurotransmitters.

There are different types of neurotransmitters and different interactions occur. Once neurotransmitters are released they are taken up by receptor sites, broken down by enzymes, or reuptaken by the axon terminal that released them. Drugs influence these interactions in different fashions. They can increase or decrease neurotransmitter synthesis. They can interfere with transport or storage of neurotransmitters. Neurotransmitters may also become blocked by drugs influencing their ability to reuptake or completely shutting down a receptor site. Drugs can slow down or speed up neurotransmitters release. They can also mimic neurotransmitters and activate receptors themselves. Finally drugs can influence how enzymes breakdown neurotransmitters.

Neurotransmitters are largely present within the brain. There are specific pathways in the brain where particular neurotransmitters dominate. Some of these consist of monoamines, neurotransmitters which have only one amine group. Some examples of monoamines are dopamine, serotonin, and norepinephrine. Two well known pathways in the brain are the nigrostriatal dopamine pathway and the mesolimbic dopamine pathway. Other important neurotransmitters in the brain are acetylcholine and GABA.

Therapeutic Index

A drug's therapeutic index is a ratio between the dose at which the drug is effective, and the dose at which it is toxic, or in other words **LD50/ED50**. The ED50 value is the **"effective dose"** for 50% of the population, or the average effective dose. The LD50 value is the **"lethal dose"** for 50% of the population. So for example, if a drug had a LD50 value of 35 mg and an ED50 value of 30 mg. It would have a therapeutic index of 30 mg/35 mg, or 1.2. The higher a drug's therapeutic index is, the safer it is. If a drug has a high therapeutic index, there is less of a chance of accidental overdose, and fewer negative symptoms at regular dosages.

How Drugs Effect Organs

Brain
The brain is the most complex organ in the human body. It functions on a higher level than the most powerful super computer. Drugs entering the body anywhere eventually find themselves in one or more of the four major arteries which serve the brain. Then the drug enters the brain through the blood-brain barrier which protects the brain by only allowing certain molecules to pass through. Unfortunately it does not block all drugs. Drugs which are similar enough in chemical structure to naturally occurring molecules pass through. Once in the brain, the drug is defused everywhere. It then interrupts normal behavior by interacting with the different neurotransmitters, receptors, and pathways according to its chemical structure.

Heart
The heart is an essential organ. It distributes blood to the different systems of the body. Drugs move throughout the body by means of the bloodstream. The rate at which the heart pumps determines how quickly drugs move around the body. Drugs can cause the heart to beat faster or slower and even cause cardiac arrest.

Lungs

The lungs are the central organ of the respiratory system. Drugs which are inhaled pass first through the lungs. The capillary walls in the lungs are very thin so the drug passes quickly into the bloodstream. The blood is then pumped through the heart and enters the brain. The drug moves relatively quickly to the brain. Also, because the drug is inhaled, its deposits do not last very long in the blood. When the drug administration stops, the drug effects stop almost immediately as well.

Intestines

Most drugs are taken orally and therefore must pass through the intestinal system. In the stomach, they are confronted by powerful acids which may break them down and reduce their potency. It is in the small intestine in which drugs are primarily absorbed. What is not absorbed is then treated by the liver and further broken down before it has a chance of reaching the brain. Another factor concerning the intestines is the amount of food already present in the system which may slow down the distribution of the drug or even completely annul it.

Liver and Kidney

The primary functions of the liver and kidney are to remove toxins from the body. Drugs are toxins and thus are removed. The kidney does some of this work, but the liver is mainly responsible for the breaking down of drugs. At times, the resulting substance is more toxic than the first because of chemical reactions with the drug and break-down enzymes. This results in a toxification of the liver. However, for the most part, the substance is detoxified and removed from the system.

Common Drug Interactions

Drugs interact with each other in many ways. It is very common for different drugs to affect each other. However, mixing drugs can be very dangerous. You should always let your doctor or pharmacist know what combination of drugs you are taking. Some of the risks of mixing drugs include a cancellation of beneficial effects of one or more drugs, unexpected side effects, and even death may result with certain combinations of drugs. Common ways for drugs to interact with each other include potentiation, summation, reduction, or cancelation. **Potentiation** is the result when two drugs combine and the resulting effects are greater than the effects of the two drugs added together. **Summation** is the result when the effects of the two drugs are simply added together. **Reduction** occurs when the drugs' effects are reduced. **Cancelation** is when the two drugs interact in such a way as to negate all effects.

With drugs easily interacting together, polydrug abuse (the abuse of multiple drugs) may occur because the affects of one drug greatly influence others. Alcohol is most commonly mixed with other drugs and often results in potentiation. Cocaethylene, a mixture of alcohol and cocaine, is twenty times more toxic than alcohol or cocaine alone. Other combinations of drugs are also dangerous. Stimulants and depressants combined do not cancel each other out. Stimulants and antidepressants have additive effects. One of the most dangerous effects of drug combination is respiratory depression which is caused by narcotics, depressants, and sedatives. When these drugs are combined chances of death are heightened.

Drug Schedule

Drugs, substances, and certain chemicals used to make drugs are classified into five (5) distinct categories or schedules depending upon the drug's acceptable medical use and the drug's abuse or dependency potential.

The abuse rate is a determinate factor in the scheduling of the drug; for example, Schedule I drugs are considered the most dangerous class of drugs with a high potential for abuse and potentially severe psychological and/or physical dependence.

As the drug schedule changes so does the abuse potential - Schedule V drugs represents the least potential for abuse.

Schedule I

Schedule I drugs, substances, or chemicals are defined as drugs with no currently accepted medical use and a high potential for abuse. Schedule I drugs are the most dangerous drugs of all the drug schedules with potentially severe psychological or physical dependence. Some examples of Schedule I drugs are:

Heroin, lysergic acid diethylamide (LSD), marijuana (cannabis), 3,4-methylenedioxymethamphetamine (ecstasy), methaqualone, and peyote.

Schedule II

Schedule II drugs, substances, or chemicals are defined as drugs with a high potential for abuse, less abuse potential than Schedule I drugs, with use potentially leading to severe psychological or physical dependence. These drugs are also considered dangerous. Some examples of Schedule II drugs are:

Cocaine, methamphetamine, methadone, hydromorphone (Dilaudid), meperidine (Demerol), oxycodone (OxyContin), fentanyl, Dexedrine, Adderall, and Ritalin.

Schedule III

Schedule III drugs, substances, or chemicals are defined as drugs with a moderate to low potential for physical and psychological dependence. Schedule III drugs abuse potential is less than Schedule I and II drugs but more than Schedule IV. Some examples of Schedule III drugs are:

Combination products with less than 15 milligrams of hydrocodone per dosage unit (Vicodin), Products containing less than 90 milligrams of codeine per dosage unit (Tylenol with codeine), ketamine, anabolic steroids, testosterone.

Schedule IV

Schedule IV drugs, substances, or chemicals are defined as drugs with a low potential for abuse and low risk of dependence. Some examples of Schedule IV drugs are:

Xanax, Soma, Darvon, Darvocet, Valium, Ativan, Talwin, Ambien.

Schedule V

Schedule V drugs, substances, or chemicals are defined as drugs with lower potential for abuse than Schedule IV and consist of preparations containing limited quantities of certain narcotics. Schedule V drugs are generally used for antidiarrheal, antitussive, and analgesic purposes. Some examples of Schedule V drugs are:

Cough medicine with less than 200 milligrams of codeine or per 100 milliliters (Robitussin AC), Lomotil, Motofen, Lyrica, Parepectolin.

Stimulants

Stimulants, sometimes referred to as "uppers," reverse the effects of fatigue on both mental and physical tasks. Two commonly used stimulants are nicotine, which is found in tobacco products, and caffeine, an active ingredient in coffee, tea, some soft drinks, and many non-prescription medicines. Used in moderation, these substances tend to relieve malaise and increase alertness. Although the use of these products has been an accepted part of U.S. culture, the recognition of their adverse effects has resulted in a proliferation of caffeine-free products and efforts to discourage cigarette smoking.

A number of stimulants, however, are under the regulatory control of the CSA. Some of these controlled substances are available by prescription for legitimate medical use in the treatment of obesity, narcolepsy, and attention deficit disorders. As drugs of abuse, stimulants are frequently taken to produce a sense of exhilaration, enhance self esteem, improve mental and physical performance, increase activity, reduce appetite, produce prolonged wakefulness, and to "get high." They are among the most potent agents of reward and reinforcement that underlie the problem of dependence.

Stimulants are also diverted from legitimate channels and clandestinely manufactured exclusively for the illicit market. They are taken orally, sniffed, smoked, and injected. Smoking, snorting, or injecting stimulants produce a sudden sensation known as a "rush" or a "flash." Abuse is often associated with a pattern of binge use – sporadically consuming large doses of stimulants over a short period of time. Heavy users may inject themselves every few hours, continuing until they have depleted their drug supply or reached a point of delirium, psychosis, and physical exhaustion. During this period of heavy use, all other interests become secondary to recreating the initial euphoric rush. Tolerance can develop rapidly, and both physical and psychological dependence occur. Abrupt cessation, even after a brief two- or three-day binge, is commonly followed by depression, anxiety, drug craving, and extreme fatigue known as a "crash."

Therapeutic levels of stimulants can produce exhilaration, extended wakefulness, and loss of appetite. These effects are greatly intensified when large doses of stimulants are taken. Physical side effects, including dizziness, tremors, headache, flushed skin, chest pain with palpitations, excessive sweating, vomiting, and abdominal cramps, may occur as a result of taking too large a dose at one time or taking large doses over an extended period of time. Psychological effects include agitation, hostility, panic, aggression, and suicidal or homicidal tendencies. Paranoia, sometimes accompanied by both auditory and visual hallucinations, may also occur. Overdose is often associated with high fever, convulsions, and cardiovascular collapse. Because accidental death is partially due to the effects of stimulants on the body's cardiovascular and temperature-regulating systems, physical exertion increases the hazards of stimulant use.

COCAINE

Cocaine, the most potent stimulant of natural origin, is extracted from the leaves of the coca plant *(Erythroxylum coca)*, which is indigenous to the Andean highlands of South America. Natives in this region chew or brew coca leaves into a tea for refreshment and to relieve fatigue, similar to the customs of chewing tobacco and drinking tea or coffee.

Pure cocaine was first isolated in the 1880s and used as a local anesthetic in eye surgery. It was particularly useful in surgery of the nose and throat because of its ability to provide anesthesia, as well as to constrict blood vessels and limit bleeding. Many of its therapeutic applications are now obsolete due to the development of safer drugs.

Illicit cocaine is usually distributed as a white crystalline powder or as an off-white chunky material. The powder, usually cocaine hydrochloride, is often diluted with a variety of substances, the most common being sugars such as lactose, inositol, and mannitol, and local anesthetics such as lidocaine. The adulteration increases the volume and thus multiplies profits. Cocaine hydrochloride is generally snorted or dissolved in water and injected. It is rarely smoked because it is heat labile (destroyed by high temperatures).

"Crack," the chunk or "rock" form of cocaine, is a ready-to-use freebase. On the illicit market, it is sold in small, inexpensive dosage units that are smoked. Smoking delivers large quantities of cocaine to the lungs, producing effects comparable to intravenous injection. Drug effects are felt almost immediately, are very intense, and are quickly over. Once introduced in the mid-1980s, crack abuse spread rapidly and made the cocaine experience available to anyone with $10 and access to a dealer. In addition to other toxicities associated with cocaine abuse, cocaine smokers suffer from acute respiratory problems including cough, shortness of breath, and severe chest pains with lung trauma and bleeding. It is noteworthy that the emergence of crack was accompanied by a dramatic increase in drug abuse problems and drug-related violence.

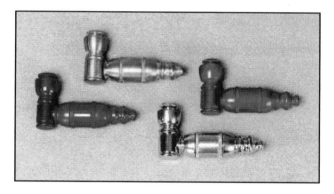

Paraphernalia used for smoking crack cocaine.

The intensity of the psychological effects of cocaine, as with most psychoactive drugs, depends on the dose and rate of entry to the brain. Cocaine reaches the brain through the snorting method in three to five minutes. Intravenous injection of cocaine produces a rush in 15 to 30 seconds, and smoking produces an almost immediate intense experience. The euphoric effects of cocaine are almost indistinguishable from those of amphetamine, although they do not last as long. These intense effects can be followed by a dysphoric crash. To avoid the fatigue and the depression of coming down, frequent repeated doses are taken. Excessive doses of cocaine may lead to seizures and death from respiratory failure, stroke, or heart failure. There is no specific antidote for cocaine overdose.

Cocaine is the second most commonly used illicit drug (following marijuana) in the United States. According to the 2003 National Survey on Drug Use and Health, more than 34 million Americans (14.7%) age 12 or older have used cocaine at least once in their lifetime. There are no drugs approved for replacement-pharmacotherapy (drugs taken on a chronic basis as a substitute for the abused drug, like methadone for heroin addiction). Cocaine addiction treatment relies heavily on psychotherapy and drugs like antidepressants to relieve some of the effects of cocaine abuse.

COCAINE: CULTIVATION TO PRODUCT

1. Coca farmers, known as "campesinos," cultivate plants throughout the Andean region of South America.

2. Depending on the method and variety of coca used, coca plants may take up to two years to mature fully.

3. Once harvested, coca leaves are sometimes allowed to dry in the sun to keep the leaves from rotting.

4. Cocaine base processors stomp the coca leaves to macerate the leaves and help extract desired alkaloids.

5. The solution is transferred by bucket to a second plastic lined pit, where lime or cement is added.

6. Gasoline is then added to the basic solution and mixed.

7. Cocaine hydrochloride (HCl) is produced through further refining and processing the cocaine base.

8. Cocaine HCl is the final product exported from South America.

9. Crack cocaine is made in the U.S. from several basic household products and cocaine HCl.

AMPHETAMINES

Amphetamine, dextroamphetamine, methamphetamine, and their various salts, are collectively referred to as amphetamines. In fact, their chemical properties and actions are so similar that even experienced users have difficulty knowing which drug they have taken.

Amphetamine was first marketed in the 1930s as Benzedrine® in an over-the-counter inhaler to treat nasal congestion. By 1937, amphetamine was available by prescription in tablet form and was used in the treatment of the sleeping disorder, narcolepsy, and the behavioral syndrome called minimal brain dysfunction, which today is called attention deficit hyperactivity disorder (ADHD). During World War II, amphetamine was widely used to keep the fighting men going and both dextroamphetamine (Dexedrine®) and methamphetamine (Methedrine®) were readily available.

As use of amphetamines spread, so did their abuse. In the 1960s, amphetamines became a perceived remedy for helping truckers to complete their long routes without falling asleep, for weight control, for helping athletes to perform better and train longer, and for treating mild depression. Intravenous amphetamines, primarily methamphetamine, were abused by a subculture known as "speed freaks." With experience, it became evident that the dangers of abuse of these drugs outweighed most of their therapeutic uses.

Increased control measures were initiated in 1965 with amendments to the federal food and drug laws to curb the black market in amphetamines. Many pharmaceutical amphetamine products were removed from the market including all injectable formulations, and doctors prescribed those that remained less freely. Recent increases in medical use of these drugs can be attributed to their use in the treatment of ADHD. Amphetamine products presently marketed include generic and brand name amphetamine (Adderall®, Dexedrine®, Dextrostat®) and brand name methamphetamine (Desoxyn®). Amphetamines are all controlled in Schedule II of the CSA.

To meet the ever-increasing black market demand for amphetamines, clandestine laboratory production has mushroomed. Today, most amphetamines distributed to the black market are produced in clandestine laboratories. Methamphetamine laboratories are, by far, the most frequently encountered clandestine laboratories in the United States. The ease of illegal synthesis, combined with tremendous profits, has resulted in significant availability of illicit methamphetamine, especially on the West Coast, where abuse of this drug has increased dramatically in recent years. Large amounts of methamphetamine are also illicitly smuggled into the United States from Mexico.

Amphetamines are generally taken orally or injected. However, the addition of "ice," the slang name for crystallized methamphetamine hydrochloride, has promoted smoking as another mode of administration. Just as "crack" is smokable cocaine, "ice" is smokable methamphetamine. Methamphetamine, in all its forms, is highly addictive and toxic.

The effects of amphetamines, especially methamphetamine, are similar to cocaine, but their onset is slower and their duration is longer. In contrast to cocaine, which is quickly removed from the brain and is almost completely metabolized, methamphetamine remains in the central nervous system longer, and a larger percentage of the drug remains unchanged in the body, producing prolonged stimulant effects. Chronic abuse produces a psychosis that resembles schizophrenia and is characterized by paranoia, picking at the skin, preoccupation with one's own thoughts, and auditory and visual hallucinations. These psychotic symptoms can persist for months and even years after use of these drugs has ceased and may be related to their neurotoxic effects. Violent and erratic behavior is frequently seen among chronic abusers of amphetamines, especially methamphetamine.

METHCATHINONE

Methcathinone, known on the streets as "Cat," is a structural analogue of methamphetamine and cathinone. Clandestinely manufactured, methcathinone is almost exclusively sold in the stable and highly water soluble hydrochloride salt form. It is most commonly snorted, although it can be taken orally by mixing it with a beverage or diluted in water and injected intravenously. Methcathinone has an abuse potential equivalent to methamphetamine and produces amphetamine-like effects. It was placed in Schedule I of the CSA in 1993.

METHYLPHENIDATE

Methylphenidate, a Schedule II substance, has a high potential for abuse and produces many of the same effects as cocaine and the amphetamines. The abuse of this substance has been documented among narcotic addicts who dissolve the tablets in water and inject the mixture. Complications arising from this practice are common due to the insoluble fillers used in the tablets. When injected, these materials block small blood vessels, causing serious damage to the lungs and retina of the eye. Binge use, psychotic episodes, cardiovascular complications, and severe psychological addiction have all been associated with methylphenidate abuse.

Methylphenidate is used legitimately in the treatment of excessive daytime sleepiness associated with narcolepsy, as is the newly marketed Schedule IV stimulant, modafinil (Provigil®). However, the primary legitimate medical use of methylphenidate (Ritalin®, Methylin®, Concerta®) is to treat attention deficit hyperactivity disorder (ADHD) in children. The increased use of this substance for the treatment of ADHD has paralleled an increase in its abuse among adolescents and young adults who crush these tablets and snort the powder to get high. Abusers have little difficulty obtaining methylphenidate from classmates or friends who have been prescribed it.

ANORECTIC DRUGS

A number of drugs have been developed and marketed to replace amphetamines as appetite suppressants. These anorectic drugs include benzphetamine (Didrex®), diethylproprion (Tenuate®, Tepanil®), mazindol (Sanorex®, Mazanor®), phendimetrazine (Bontril®, Prelu-27®), and phentermine (Lonamin®, Fastin®, Adipex®). These substances are in Schedule III or IV of the CSA and produce some amphetamine-like effects. Of these diet pills, phentermine is the most widely prescribed and most frequently encountered on the illicit market. Two Schedule IV anorectics often used in combination with phentermine, fenfluramine and dexfenfluramine, were removed from the U.S. market because they were associated with heart valve problems.

KHAT

For centuries, khat, the fresh young leaves of the *Catha edulis* shrub, has been consumed where the plant is cultivated, primarily East Africa and the Arabian Peninsula. There, chewing khat predates the use of coffee and is used in a similar social context. Chewed in moderation, khat alleviates fatigue and reduces appetite. Compulsive use may result in manic behavior with grandiose

Harvested Khat plants.

delusions or in a paranoid type of illness, sometimes accompanied by hallucinations. Khat has been smuggled into the United States and other countries from the source countries for use by emigrants. It contains a number of chemicals, among which are two controlled substances, cathinone (Schedule I) and cathine (Schedule IV). As the leaves mature or dry, cathinone is converted to cathine, which significantly reduces its stimulatory properties.

ST. JOHN'S WORT

St. John's Wort is a herbal medicine used for treating mild depression. While few side effects are present with the drug, there are many drugs that interact with is. Women taking birth control pills should not use it. In the United States it is an over the counter drug, few countries requiring a prescription.

Depressants

Historically, people of almost every culture have used chemical agents to induce sleep, relieve stress, and allay anxiety. While alcohol is one of the oldest and most universal agents used for these purposes, hundreds of substances have been developed that produce central nervous system depression. These drugs have been referred to as downers, sedatives, hypnotics, minor tranquilizers, anxiolytics, and anti-anxiety medications. Unlike most other classes of drugs of abuse, depressants are rarely produced in clandestine laboratories. Generally, legitimate pharmaceutical products are diverted to the illicit market. A notable exception to this is a relatively recent drug of abuse, gamma hydroxybutyric acid (GHB).

Choral hydrate and paraldehyde are two of the oldest pharmaceutical depressants still in use today. Other depressants, including gluthethimide, methaqualone, and meprobamate, have been important players in the milieu of depressant use and abuse. However, two major groups of depressants have dominated the licit and illicit market for nearly a century, first barbiturates and now benzodiazepines.

Barbiturates were very popular in the first half of the 20th century. In moderate amounts, these drugs produce a state of intoxication that is remarkably similar to alcohol intoxication. Symptoms include slurred speech, loss of motor coordination, and impaired judgment. Depending on the dose, frequency, and duration of use, one can rapidly develop tolerance, and physical and psychological dependence on barbiturates. With the development of tolerance, the margin of safety between the effective dose and the lethal dose becomes very narrow. That is, in order to obtain the same level of intoxication, the tolerant abuser may raise his or her dose to a level that may result in coma or death. Although many individuals have taken barbiturates therapeutically without harm, concern about the addiction potential of barbiturates and the ever-increasing number of fatalities associated with them led to the development of alternative medications. Today, less than 10 percent of all depressant prescriptions in the United States are for barbiturates.

Benzodiazepines were first marketed in the 1960s. Touted as much safer depressants with far less addiction potential than barbiturates, today these drugs account for about one out of every five prescriptions for controlled substances. Although benzodiazepines produce significantly less respiratory depression than barbiturates, it is now recognized that benzodiazepines share many of the undesirable side effects of the barbiturates. A number of toxic central nervous system effects are seen with chronic high-dose benzodiazepine therapy, including headaches, irritability, confusion, memory impairment, and depression. The risk of developing over-sedation, dizziness, and confusion increases substantially with higher doses of benzodiazepines. Prolonged use can lead to physical dependence even at doses recommended for medical treatment. Unlike barbiturates, large doses of benzodiazepines are rarely fatal unless combined with other drugs or alcohol. Although primary abuse of benzodiazepines is well documented, abuse of these drugs usually occurs as part of a pattern of multiple drug abuse. For example, heroin or cocaine abusers will use benzodiazepines and other depressants to augment their "high" or alter the side effects associated with over-stimulation or narcotic withdrawal.

There are marked similarities among the withdrawal symptoms seen with most drugs classified as depressants. In the mildest form, the withdrawal syndrome may produce insomnia and anxiety, usually the same symptoms that initiated the drug use. With a greater level of dependence, tremors and weakness are also present, and in its most severe form, the withdrawal syndrome can cause seizures and delirium. Unlike the withdrawal syndrome seen with most other drugs of abuse, withdrawal from depressants can be life threatening.

BARBITURATES

Barbiturates are classified as drugs which depress a person's system. They are grouped in three types, based on how fast acting they are. The first group, short acting, takes effect very quickly. Usually within around 20 minutes. They are generally used as types of anesthesia. The second group, intermediate acting, take longer to take effect, but last for a longer time. For example, an intermediate barbiturate may not take effect for 30 minutes, but will last for 6 hours. The third group is long acting. These drugs take hours or days to take effect, but are used long term, for example anxiety medication. Barbiturates have been replaced over time by benzodiazepines because of their addictive properties, and because they have more severe effects when overdose occurs.

Barbiturates were first introduced for medical use in the early 1900s. More than 2,500 barbiturates have been synthesized, and at the height of their popularity, about 50 were marketed for human use. Today, about a dozen are in medical use. Barbiturates produce a wide spectrum of central nervous system depression, from mild sedation to coma, and have been used as sedatives, hypnotics, anesthetics, and anticonvulsants. The primary differences among many of these products are how fast they produce an effect and how long those effects last. Barbiturates are classified as ultrashort, short, intermediate, and long-acting.

The ultrashort-acting barbiturates produce anesthesia within about one minute after intravenous administration. Those in current medical use are the Schedule IV drug methohexital (Brevital®), and the Schedule III drugs thiamyl (Surital®) and thiopental (Pentothal®). Barbiturate abusers prefer the Schedule II short-acting and intermediate-acting barbiturates that include amobarbital (Amytal®), pentobarbital (Nembutal®), secobarbital (Seconal®), and Tuinal (an amobarbital/secobarbital combination product). Other short and intermediate-acting barbiturates are in Schedule III and include butalbital (Fiorina®), butabarbital (Butisol®), talbutal (Lotusate®), and aprobarbital (Alurate®). After oral administration, the onset of action is from 15 to 40 minutes, and the effects last up to six hours. These drugs are primarily used for insomnia and preoperative sedation. Veterinarians use pentobarbital for anesthesia and euthanasia.

Long-acting barbiturates include phenobarbital (Luminal®) and mephobarbital (Mebaral®), both of which are in Schedule IV. Effects of these drugs are realized in about one hour and last for about 12 hours, and are used primarily for daytime sedation and the treatment of seizure disorders.

BENZODIAZEPINES

The benzodiazepine family of depressants is used therapeutically to produce sedation, induce sleep, relieve anxiety and muscle spasms, and to prevent seizures. In general, benzodiazepines act as hypnotics in high doses, anxiolytics in moderate doses, and sedatives in low doses. Of the drugs marketed in the United States that affect central nervous system function, benzodiazepines are among the most widely prescribed medications. Fifteen members of this group are presently marketed in the United States, and about 20 additional benzodiazepines are marketed in other countries. Benzodiazepines are controlled in Schedule IV of the CSA.

Short-acting benzodiazepines are generally used for patients with sleep-onset insomnia (difficulty falling asleep) without daytime anxiety. Shorter-acting benzodiazepines used to manage insomnia include estazolam (ProSom®), flurazepam (Dalmane®), temazepam (Restoril®), and triazolam (Halcion®). Midazolam (Versed®), a short-acting benzodiazepine, is utilized for sedation, or treating anxiety and amnesia in critical care settings and prior to anesthesia. It is available in the United States as an injectable preparation and as a syrup (primarily for pediatric patients).

Benzodiazepines with a longer duration of action are utilized to treat insomnia in patients with daytime anxiety. These benzodiazepines include alprazolam (Xanax®), chlordiazepoxide (Librium®), clorazepate (Tranxene®), diazepam (Valium®), halazepam (Paxipam®), lorzepam (Ativan®), oxazepam (Serax®), prazepam (Centrax®), and quazepam (Doral®). Clonazepam (Klonopin®), diazepam, and clorazepate are also used as anticonvulsants.

Klonopin 1mg

Klonopin 0.50mg

Benzodiazepines are classified in the CSA as depressants. Repeated use of large doses or, in some cases, daily use of therapeutic doses of benzodiazepines is associated with amnesia, hostility, irritability, and vivid or disturbing dreams, as well as tolerance and physical dependence. The withdrawal syndrome is similar to that of alcohol and may require hospitalization. Abrupt cessation of benzodiazepines is not recommended and tapering-down the dose eliminates many of the unpleasant symptoms of withdrawal.

Given the millions of prescriptions written for benzodiazepines, relatively few individuals increase their dose on their own initiative or engage in drug-seeking behavior. Those individuals who do abuse benzodiazepines often maintain their drug supply by getting prescriptions from several doctors, forging prescriptions, or buying diverted pharmaceutical products on the illicit market. Abuse is frequently associated with adolescents and young adults who take benzodiazepines to obtain a "high." This intoxicated state results in reduced inhibition and impaired judgment. Concurrent use of alcohol or other depressant with benzodiazepines can be life threatening. Abuse of benzodiazepines is particularly high among heroin and cocaine abusers. A large percentage of people entering treatment for narcotic or cocaine addiction also report abusing benzodiazepines. Alprazolam and diazepam are the two most frequently encountered benzodiazepines on the illicit market.

Benzodiazepines are any type of drug which is used to counter anxiety. Examples include Valium, Xanax, and Ativan. Benzodiazepines are considered to be the most abused pharmaceutical drug. Although benzodiazepines overdoses do not generally cause severe complications, it is unwise to do so. Benzodiazepines work by decreasing brain function, and as the dose increases so do the side effects. For example, side effects of benzodiazepines include drowsiness, dizziness, depression, nausea, memory loss, confusion, and blurred vision.

FLUNITRAZEPAM

Flunitrazepam (Rohypnol®) is a benzodiazepine that is not manufactured or legally marketed in the United States, but is smuggled in by traffickers. In the mid-1990s, flunitrazepam was extensively trafficked in Florida and Texas. Known as "rophies," "roofies," and "roach," flunitrazepam gained popularity among younger individuals as a "party" drug. It has also been utilized as a "date rape" drug. In this context, flunitrazepam is placed in the alcoholic drink of an unsuspecting victim to incapacitate them and prevent resistance from sexual assault. The victim is frequently unaware of what has happened to them and often does not report the incident to authorities. A number of actions by the manufacturer of this drug and by government agencies have resulted in reducing the availability and abuse of flunitrazepam in the United States.

LUNESTA

Eszopiclone, better known as Lunesta® is a FDA approved nonbenzodiazepine hypnotic used to treat insomnia, primarily with the issue of falling asleep.

GAMMA HYDROXYBUTYRIC ACID (GHB)

In recent years, *gamma* hydroxybutyric acid (GHB) has emerged as a significant drug of abuse throughout the United States. Abusers of this drug fall into three major groups: (1) users who take GHB for its intoxicant or euphoriant effects; (2) bodybuilders who abuse GHB for its alleged utility as an anabolic agent or as a sleep aid; and (3) individuals who use GHB as a weapon for sexual assault. These categories are not mutually exclusive and an abuser may use the drug illicitly to produce several effects. GHB is frequently taken with alcohol or other drugs that heighten its effects and is often found at bars, nightclubs, rave parties, and gyms. Teenagers and young adults who frequent these establishments are the primary users. Like flunitrazepam, GHB is often referred to as a "date-rape" drug. GHB involvement in rape cases is likely to be unreported or unsubstantiated because GHB is quickly eliminated from the body making detection in body fluids unlikely. Its fast onset of depressant effects may render the victim with little memory of the details of the attack.

GHB produces a wide range of central nervous system effects, including dose-dependent drowsiness, dizziness, nausea, amnesia, visual hallucinations, hypertension, bradycardia, severe respiratory depression, and coma. The use of alcohol in combination with GHB greatly enhances its depressant effects. Overdose frequently requires emergency room care, and many GHB-related fatalities have been reported.

Gamma butyrolactone (GBL) and 1, 4-butanediol are GHB analogues that can be used as substitutes for GHB. When ingested, these analogues are converted to GHB and produce identical effects. GBL is also used in the clandestine production of GHB as an immediate precursor. Both GBL and 1, 4-butanediol have been sold at health food stores and on various internet sites.

The abuse of GHB began to seriously escalate in the mid-1990s. For example, in 1994, there were 55 emergency department episodes involving GHB reported in the Drug Abuse Warning Network (DAWN) system. By 2002, there were 3,330 emergency room episodes. DAWN data also indicated that most users were male, less than 25 years of age, and taking the drug orally for recreational use.

GHB was placed in Schedule I of the CSA in March 2000. *Gamma* butyrolactone (GBL) was made a List I Chemical in February 2000. GHB has recently been approved as a medication (Xyrem®) for the treatment of cataplexy associated with some types of narcolepsy. This approved medication is in Schedule III of the CSA.

PARALDEHYDE

Paraldehyde (Paral®) is a Schedule IV depressant used most frequently in hospital settings to treat delirium tremens associated with alcohol withdrawal. Many individuals who become addicted to paraldehyde have been initially exposed during treatment for alcoholism and, despite the disagreeable odor and taste, come to prefer it to alcohol. This drug is not used by injection because of tissue damage, and taken orally, it can be irritating to the throat and stomach. One of the signs of paraldehyde use is a strong, characteristic smell to the breath.

CHLORAL HYDRATE

The oldest of the hypnotic (sleep inducing) depressants, chloral hydrate was first synthesized in 1832. Marketed as syrups or soft gelatin capsules, chloral hydrate takes effect in a relatively short time (30 minutes) and will induce sleep in about an hour. A solution of chloral hydrate and alcohol constituted the infamous "knockout drops" or "Mickey Finn." At therapeutic doses, chloral hydrate has little effect on respiration and blood pressure; however, a toxic dose produces severe respiratory depression and very low blood pressure. Chronic use is associated with liver damage and a severe withdrawal syndrome. Although some physicians consider chloral hydrate to be the drug of choice for sedation of children before diagnostic, dental, or medical procedures, its general use as a hypnotic has declined. Chloral hydrate, Noctec®, and other compounds, preparations, or mixtures containing choral hydrate are in Schedule IV of the CSA.

GLUTETHIMIDE AND METHAQUALONE

Glutethimide (Doriden®) was introduced in 1954 and methaqualone (Quaalude®, Sopor®) in 1965 as safe barbiturate substitutes. Experience demonstrated, however, that their addiction liability and the severity of withdrawal symptoms were similar to those of barbiturates. By 1972, "luding out," taking methaqualone with wine, was a popular college pastime. Excessive use leads to tolerance, dependence, and withdrawal symptoms similar to those of barbiturates. In the United States, the marketing of methaqualone pharmaceutical products stopped in 1984, and methaqualone was transferred to Schedule I of the CSA. In 1991, glutethimide was transferred into Schedule II in response to an upsurge in the prevalence of diversion, abuse, and overdose deaths. Today, there is little medical use of glutethimide in the United States.

MEPROBAMATE

Meprobamate was introduced as an anti-anxiety agent in 1955 and is prescribed primarily to treat anxiety, tension, and associated muscle spasms. More than 50 tons are distributed annually in the United States under its generic name and brand names such as Miltown® and Equanil®.

Its onset and duration of action are similar to the intermediate-acting barbiturates; however, therapeutic doses of meprobamate produce less sedation and toxicity than barbiturates. Excessive use can result in psychological and physical dependence. Carisoprodol (Soma®), a skeletal muscle relaxant, is metabolized to meprobamate. This conversion may account for some of the properties associated with carisoprodol and likely contributes to its abuse.

NEWLY MARKETED DRUGS

Zolpidem (Ambien®) and zaleplon (Sonata®) are two relatively new, benzodiazepine-like CNS depressants that have been approved for the short-term treatment of insomnia. Both of these drugs share many of the same properties as the benzodiazepines and are in Schedule IV of the CSA.

VALIUM

Valium, also known as diazepam, is commonly used as a relaxant. It is used for anxiety, muscle spasms, insomnia, alcohol withdrawal, seizures, and other situations. Valium belongs to a bigger group of drugs called benzodiazepines, which are considered to be the most abused pharmaceutical drugs.

XANAX

Xanax, also known as alprazolam, is mainly used to treat anxiety disorders. It belongs to a group of drugs called benzodiazepines, which are relaxants. It has a relatively fast onset, and is considered the most abused of the Benzodiazepines. It has sedative, hypnotic, and muscle relaxant properties.

KAVA KAVA

Kava kava has been used as a ceremonial drink in the Pacific Islands. Its effects on the body are similar to alcohol, providing a relaxing and calming effect. This is used to treat insomnia or anxiety.

The roots of the plant can be ground, ingested and used to make a tea or drink. Because of concerns over severe liver damage, kava should only be used under a doctor's discretion although it is currently available in the U.S. as an over the counter drug.

Alcohol

Alcohol is a depressant that comes from organic sources including grapes, grains and berries. These are fermented or are distilled into a liquid.

Alcohol affects every part of the body. It is carried through the bloodstream to the brain, stomach, internal organs, liver, kidneys, muscles – everywhere. It is absorbed very quickly (as fast as 5-10 minutes) and can stay in the body for several hours.

Alcohol affects the central nervous system and brain. It can make users loosen up, relax, and feel more comfortable or can make them more aggressive.

Unfortunately, it also lowers their inhibitions, which can set them up for dangerous or embarrassing behavior. Alcohol is a drug and is only legal for people over the age 21.

According to the Substance Abuse and Mental Health Services Administration (SAMHSA), 2.6 million young people do not know that a person can die of an overdose of alcohol. Alcohol poisoning occurs when a person drinks a large quantity of alcohol in a short amount of time.

LD50 is a term in toxicology. It refers to the lethal dose of alcohol to the median population, or in other words, what is the lethal dose for 50% of the population. **The LD50 for alcohol is .45% BAC (blood alcohol concentration).**

🎓 *Alcohol Health Hazards*

People who begin drinking before the age of 15 are four times more likely to develop alcohol dependence than those who wait until age 21. Each additional year of delayed drinking onset reduces the probability of alcohol dependence by 14 percent.

Adolescents who drink heavily assume the same long-term health risks as adults who drink heavily. This means they are at increased risk of developing cirrhosis of the liver, pancreatitis, hemorrhagic stroke, and certain forms of cancer.

Adolescents who use alcohol are more likely to become sexually active, which places them at greater risk of HIV infection and other sexually transmitted diseases.

One study showed that students diagnosed with alcohol abuse were four times more likely to experience major depression than those without an alcohol problem. Alcohol use among adolescents has been associated with considering, planning, attempting, and completing suicide.

Binge drinking, drinking just to become intoxicated, is becoming more and more problematic. Binge drinking averages at five drinks for a man in a single sitting or four drinks at a sitting.

Ethyl alcohol or ethanol is what makes beer, wine, and liquor intoxicating. There are two main ways to create alcohol. The first is fermentation, where plant sugars are broken down by yeast organisms, creating alcohol and carbon dioxide. This creates a mash. Manufacturers then add other ingredients that dilute the alcohol in the beverage. Other beverages are created with an additional step called distillation – where alcoholic vapors are released from the mash when heated to high temperatures. **Proof** is the alcohol percentage in the beverage. To figure out the percentage of alcohol in a drink, simply divide the proof by half. For example, 80 proof vodka is 40% alcohol by volume. Most wines are between 12-15% and most beers (depending on state) are between 2-6%.

The liver is affected by alcohol more than any other organ. The liver is the organ which metabolizes alcohol once it has been consumed. There are three major alcoholic liver diseases (ALD's) which are caused by consuming alcohol. These diseases are fatty liver, alcoholic hepatitis, and cirrhosis. Fatty liver is the least serious. It occurs after acute alcohol ingestion and is reversible if the person does not drink again for a while. Alcoholic hepatitis is caused by inflammation in the liver, which occurs because of excessive drinking. If the person stops drinking, it is possibly reversible. However, if the person continues drinking excessively it will often progress to cirrhosis. Cirrhosis is the most serious of the three diseases. It is when the liver cells become damaged and die, becoming scar tissue. The death of liver cells is not reversible and once cells have died, cirrhosis is not curable. As the amount of scar tissue increases, liver function decreases. This results in the build up of toxins in the system and eventually death.

Blood-alcohol concentration (BAC) is the ratio of alcohol to the total blood volume. Alcohol is a diuretic, causing increased trips to the bathroom. It also causes dehydration. You also should be careful of potential drug interaction. Some medications, even over-the-counter, should not be taken with alcohol and vice-versa.

The formula for estimated blood alcohol content (BAC) is

$$BAC = NSD \times .03 - NHD \times .02$$

NSD stands for number of standards drinks, and NHD stands for number of hours since drinking began. This formula is used because the liver metabolizes alcohol at a steady rate, so by setting up a formula which relates the amount a person has been drinking, and how much alcohol they consume, their BAC can be estimated. For example if a person has 4 standard drinks in 2 hours their BAC will be 4(.03)-1(.02)=.10 percent. In the United States, the legal limit for driving is .08 percent, so the person in this example would not be allowed to drive.

Long term effects include:
- High cholesterol
- Liver disease – the cirrhosis or hardening of the liver
- Alcoholic hepatitis
- Cancer of the throat, stomach, mouth, tongue, breast and liver
- Chronic inflammation of the pancreas

You get the same amount of alcohol whether you drink:

    1 bottle (12 oz.) beer
    1 1/5 bottles (14.4 oz.) "light" beer (4% alcohol)
    1 bottle (12 oz.) of cooler (wine, spirit or beer with around 5% alcohol)
    1 glass (3 oz.) sherry
    1 glass (5 oz.) table wine
    1 shot (1 ½ oz.) liquor (rye, gin, rum or Scotch)

Though there are many myths about how to get sober quickly, the only thing which gets alcohol out of a person's system is time. The liver must metabolize alcohol in order for it to be eliminated from the body. This occurs at a rate of .6 oz per hour, which is the approximate amount of alcohol in one drink.

The liver metabolizes alcohol by converting into a form that it can break down more easily. The conversion depends on an enzyme called alcohol dehydrogenase (ADH) which is found in high quantities in the liver. Through the conversion, the alcohol is detoxified and removed from the blood.

Alcohol Treatment

There are many types of treatment programs including:
- Private treatment facilities
- Family, individual and group therapy (think Alcoholics Anonymous)
- Drug and aversion therapy (when the drugs you are taking mix with alcohol, headache, nausea, drowsiness and other hangover symptoms appear)

Korsakoff's Syndrome

Korsakoff's syndrome is caused by a thiamine (vitamin B) deficiency in the brain. It can be caused by malnutrition, but it is also associated with severe alcoholism. Symptoms of Korsakoff's syndrome include anterograde amnesia, retrograde amnesia, and confabulation. Anterograde amnesia is an inability to form lasting memories. Retrograde amnesia is losing past memories, and confabulation is when a person "creates" memories and believes them to be real.

Fetal Alcohol Syndrome

When a pregnant woman drinks alcohol, so does her unborn baby. There is no known safe amount of alcohol to drink while pregnant and there also does not appear to be a safe time to drink during pregnancy either. Therefore, it is recommended that women abstain from drinking alcohol at any time during pregnancy. Women who are sexually active and do not use effective birth control should also refrain from drinking because they could become pregnant and not know for several weeks or more. **The first trimester of a pregnancy is the most dangerous for the fetus in regard to alcohol or drug use.**

FAS is the severe end of a spectrum of effects that can occur when a woman drinks during pregnancy. Fetal death is the most extreme outcome. FAS is a disorder characterized by abnormal facial features and growth and central nervous system (CNS) problems. If a pregnant woman drinks alcohol but her child does not have all of the symptoms of FAS, it is possible that her child has another FASD, such as alcohol-related neurodevelopmental disorder (ARND). Children with ARND do not have full FAS but might demonstrate learning and behavioral problems caused by prenatal exposure to alcohol. Examples of these problems are difficulties with mathematical skills, difficulties with memory or attention, poor school performance, and poor impulse control and/or judgment.

Children with FASDs might have the following characteristics or exhibit the following behaviors:
- Small size for gestational age or small stature in relation to peers
- Facial abnormalities such as small eye openings
- Poor coordination
- Hyperactive behavior
- Learning disabilities
- Developmental disabilities (e.g., speech and language delays)
- Mental retardation or low IQ
- Problems with daily living
- Poor reasoning and judgment skills
- Sleep and sucking disturbances in infancy

Children with FASDs are at risk for psychiatric problems, criminal behavior, unemployment, and incomplete education. These are secondary conditions that an individual is not born with but might acquire as a result of FAS or a related disorder. These conditions can be very serious, but there are protective factors that have been found to help individuals with FASDs. For example, a child who is diagnosed early in life can be placed in appropriate educational classes and given access to social services that can help the child and his or her family.

Alcohol Regulations

In 1920, the US Congress passed the 18th amendment to the Constitution. It prohibited the production, sale, transport, and import of alcohol within the entire United States. This amendment was passed because of the major problems that were associated with drinking, especially seen in saloons in the West. This amendment was a victory for the Saloon League and the Women's Christian Temperance Union (WCTU) who had long been fighting for reform. This amendment helped reduce drinking, but also changed the problems associated with alcohol from saloons to organized crime, who took over the alcohol industry. However, prohibition was short lived and ended in 1933 with the 21st amendment which repealed the 18th and put states in control of regulating alcohol.

Tobacco

The following are the different types of tobacco:
- Snuff: A powdered form of tobacco snorted through the nose or held in the mouth between the gum and the cheek.
- Chewing Tobacco: A stringy type of tobacco that is held in the mouth then chewed and sucked.
- Cigarettes: Tobacco rolled in paper then smoked.
- Clove Cigarettes: Cigarettes that are made up of 40% ground cloves and 60% tobacco. Many people mistakenly believe that these cigarettes actually give you a higher dosage of cancer-causing chemicals.
- Cigars: Simply tobacco that is wrapped in more tobacco.

Although many of the chemicals in cigarettes have been tested for safety, they haven't been tested after having been burned. Many of the chemicals in cigarettes become more dangerous when burned. Over 4,000 chemicals are released when a cigarette is burned, including at least 46 carcinogens, or cancer causing chemicals. Chemicals in cigarettes include nicotine, tar, formaldehyde, carbon monoxide, ammonia, arsenic, and hydrogen cyanide.

Tar is a thick brownish substance, condensed from the matter in smoked tobacco, that forms in the lungs.

Carbon Monoxide is a toxic gas found in cigarette smoke.

Nicotine is the stimulant in tobacco products. It is a very powerful stimulant that produces a multitude of physiological effects.

Use of tobacco can result in many diseases including:
- Lung cancer
- Emphysema
- Buerger's disease (reduction of blood to the extremities, particularly the feet)

 Cannabis

Cannabis is the plant which marijuana is made from. It is classified into three different groups, all of which have psychoactive properties. They are cannabis sativa (C. sativa), cannabis indica (C. indica), and cannabis ruderalis (C. ruderalis).

Cannabis sativa L., the cannabis plant, grows wild throughout most of the tropic and temperate regions of the world. Prior to the advent of synthetic fibers, the cannabis plant was cultivated for the tough fiber of its stem. In the United States, cannabis is legitimately grown only for scientific research.

Cannabis contains chemicals called cannabinoids that are unique to the cannabis plant. Among the cannabinoids synthesized by the plant are cannabinol, cannabidiol, cannabinolidic acids, cannabigerol, cannabichromene, and several isomers of tetrahydrocannabinol. One of these, delta-9-tetrahydrocannabinol (THC), is believed to be responsible for most of the characteristic psychoactive effects of cannabis. Research has resulted in development and marketing of the dronabinol (synthetic THC) product, Marinol®, for the control of nausea and vomiting caused by chemotheraputic agents used in the treatment of cancer and to stimulate appetite in AIDS patients. Marinol® was rescheduled in 1999 and placed in Schedule III of the CSA.

Cannabis products are usually smoked. Their effects are felt within minutes, reach their peak in 10 to 30 minutes, and may linger for two or three hours. The effects experienced often depend upon the experience and expectations of the individual user, as well as the activity of the drug itself. Low doses tend to induce a sense of well-being and a dreamy state of relaxation, which may be accompanied by a more vivid sense of sight, smell, taste, and hearing, as well as by subtle alterations in thought formation and expression. This state of intoxication may not be noticeable to an observer. However, driving, occupational, or household accidents may result from a distortion of time and space relationships and impaired motor coordination. Stronger doses intensify reactions. The individual may experience shifting sensory imagery, rapidly fluctuating emotions, fragmentary thoughts with disturbing associations, an altered sense of self-identity, impaired memory, and a dulling of attention despite an illusion of heightened insight. High doses may result in image distortion, a loss of personal identity, fantasies, and hallucinations.

Three drugs that come from cannabis – marijuana, hashish, and hashish oil – are distributed on the U.S. illicit market. Having no currently accepted medical use in treatment in the United States, they remain under Schedule I of the CSA. Today, cannabis is illicitly cultivated, both indoors and out, to maximize its THC content, thereby producing the greatest possible psychoactive effect.

MARIJUANA

Marijuana is the most frequently encountered illicit drug worldwide. In the United States, according to the 2003 Monitoring the Future Study, 57 percent of adults aged 19 to 28 reported having used marijuana in their lifetime. Among younger Americans, 17.5 percent of 8th graders and 46.1 percent of 12th graders had used marijuana in their lifetime. The term "marijuana," as commonly used, refers to the leaves and flowering tops of the cannabis plant that are dried to produce a tobacco-like substance. Marijuana varies significantly in its potency, depending on the source and selection of plant materials used. The form of marijuana known as sinsemilla (Spanish, sin semilla: without seed), derived from the unpollinated female cannabis plant, is preferred for its high THC content. Marijuana is usually smoked in the form of loosely rolled cigarettes called joints, bongs, or hollowed out commercial cigars called blunts. Joints and blunts may be laced with a number of adulterants including phencyclidine (PCP), substantially altering the effects and toxicity of these products. Street names for marijuana include pot, grass, weed, Mary Jane, and reefer. Although marijuana grown in the United States was once considered inferior because of a low concentration of THC, advancements in plant selection and cultivation have resulted in higher THC-containing domestic marijuana. In 1974, the average THC content of illicit marijuana was less than one percent. Today most commercial grade marijuana from Mexico/Columbia and domestic outdoor cultivated marijuana has an average THC content of about 4 to 6 percent. Between 1998 and 2002, NIDA-sponsored Marijuana Potency Monitoring System (MPMP) analyzed 4,603 domestic samples. Of those samples, 379 tested over 15 percent THC, 69 samples tested between 20 and 25 percent THC and four samples tested over 25 percent THC.

Marijuana contains known toxins and cancer-causing chemicals. Marijuana users experience the same health problems as tobacco smokers, such as bronchitis, emphysema, and bronchial asthma. Some of the effects of marijuana use also include increased heart rate, dryness of the mouth, reddening of the eyes, impaired motor skills and concentration, and hunger with an increased desire for sweets. Extended use increases risk to the lungs and reproductive system, as well as suppression of the immune system. Occasionally, hallucinations, fantasies, and paranoia are reported. Long-term chronic marijuana use is associated with an Amotivational Syndrome characterized by: apathy; impairment of judgment, memory and concentration; and loss of interest in personal appearance and pursuit of goals.

The most commonly used illegal drug is marijuana. There are over 2,000 chemicals introduced to the body through smoking marijuana. Marijuana has different effects on different people. For example, some people feel very relaxed, while others are panicked and violent. Marijuana is a Schedule I drug, and is illegal in the United States except (in some states) when users have a prescription. This seems to conflict with the information that Marijuana is a Schedule I drug with no medicinal purpose, but for the purposes of this test, it is still a Schedule I drug.

Symptoms of Marijuana withdrawal include:

- Anger
- Irritibility
- Depression
- Restlessness
- Weight loss
- Anxiety
- Insomnia
- Nervousness
- Headache
- Stomach ache
- Increased sweating
- Fever
- Chills
- Shakiness

Most users experience withdrawal symptoms within the first week of abstinence from the drug. About half of users that use the drug three or more times a week experienced at least two of the symptoms.

HASHISH

Hashish consists of the THC-rich resinous material of the cannabis plant, which is collected, dried, and then compressed into a variety of forms, such as balls, cakes, or cookie-like sheets. Pieces are then broken off, placed in pipes, and smoked. The Middle East, North Africa, and Pakistan/Afghanistan are the main sources of hashish. The THC content of hashish that reached the United States, where demand is limited, averaged about five percent in the 1990s.

HASHISH OIL

The term "hash oil" is used by illicit drug users and dealers, but is a misnomer in suggesting any resemblance to hashish. Hash oil is produced by extracting the cannabinoids from plant material with a solvent. The color and odor of the resulting extract will vary, depending on the type of solvent used. Current samples of hash oil, a viscous liquid ranging from amber to dark brown in color, average about 15 percent THC. In terms of its psychoactive effect, a drop or two of this liquid on a cigarette is equal to a single "joint" of marijuana.

Inhalants

Inhalants are common products found right in the home and are among the most popular and deadly substances kids abuse. Inhalant abuse can result in death from the very first use. About one in five kids report having used inhalants by the eighth grade. Teens use inhalants by sniffing or "snorting" fumes from containers; spraying aerosols directly into the mouth or nose; bagging, by inhaling a substance inside a paper or plastic bag; huffing from an inhalant-soaked rag; or inhaling from balloons filled with nitrous oxide.

Inhalants are breathable chemical vapors that produce psychoactive (mind-altering) effects. Although people are exposed to volatile solvents and other inhalants in the home and in the workplace, many do not think of "inhalable" substances as drugs because most of them were never meant to be used in that way.

Young people are likely to abuse inhalants, in part, because inhalants are readily available and inexpensive. Parents should see that these substances are monitored closely so that children do not abuse them.

Inhalants fall into the following categories:

SOLVENTS

- industrial or household solvents or solvent-containing products, including paint thinners or solvents, degreasers (dry-cleaning fluids), gasoline, and glues
- art or office supply solvents, including correction fluids, felt-tip-marker fluid, and electronic contact cleaners

GASES

- gases used in household or commercial products, including butane lighters and propane tanks, whipping cream aerosols or dispensers (whippets), and refrigerant gases
- household aerosol propellants and associated solvents in items such as spray paints, hair or deodorant sprays, and fabric protector sprays
- medical anesthetic gases, such as ether, chloroform, halothane, and nitrous oxide (laughing gas)

NITRITES

- aliphatic nitrites, including cyclohexyl nitrite, which is available to the general public; amyl nitrite, which is available only by prescription; and butyl nitrite, which is now an illegal substance

INHALANT HEALTH HAZARDS

Short Term Effects

Nearly all abused inhalants produce effects similar to anesthetics, which act to slow down the body's functions. When inhaled in sufficient concentrations, inhalants can cause intoxicating effects that can last only a few minutes or several hours if inhalants are taken repeatedly. Initially, users may feel slightly stimulated; with successive inhalations, they may feel less inhibited and less in control; finally, a user can lose consciousness.

Irreversible Hazards

Inhalants are toxic. Chronic exposure can lead to brain damage or nerve damage similar to multiple sclerosis; damage to the heart, lungs, liver and kidneys; and prolonged abuse can affect thinking, movement, vision and hearing.

Sniffing highly concentrated amounts of the chemicals in solvents or aerosol sprays can directly induce heart failure and death. Heart failure results from the chemicals interfering with the heart's rhythm-regulating system, causing the heart to stop beating. This is especially common from the abuse of fluorocarbons and butane-type gases. High concentrations of inhalants also cause death from asphyxiation, suffocation, convulsions or seizures, coma, choking or fatal injury from accidents while intoxicated. Other irreversible effects caused by inhaling specific solvents are:

- Hearing loss - toluene (paint sprays, glues, dewaxers) and trichloroethylene (cleaning fluids, correction fluids)
- Peripheral neuropathies or limb spasms - hexane (glues, gasoline) and nitrous oxide (whipping cream, gas cylinders)
- Central nervous system or brain damage - toluene (paint sprays, glues, dewaxers)
- Bone marrow damage - benzene (gasoline)
- Liver and kidney damage - toluene- containing substances and chlorinated hydrocarbons (correction fluids, dry-cleaning fluids)
- Blood oxygen depletion - organic nitrites ("poppers," "bold," and "rush") and methylene chloride (varnish removers, paint thinners)

Physical signs of inhalant use:
- Unusual breath odor or chemical odor on clothing
- Spots and/or sores around the mouth
- Nausea and/or loss of appetite

- Slurred or disoriented speech
- Drunk, dazed or dizzy appearance
- Red or runny eyes or nose

Why do young people use inhalants instead of other drugs?
The products are widely available, inexpensive, easy to conceal and legal. Most users do not realize how dangerous inhalants can be. Many young people start because they don't think these substances can hurt them. Once hooked, they find it a tough habit to break.

Who is at risk for using inhalants?
Inhalants are second only to marijuana in terms of adolescent drug use, and all kids are at risk. Youth drug use cuts across all geographic, socio-economic, racial and ethnic boundaries.

Prevention
Parents can keep their teens away from inhalants by talking to them and letting them know the dangers of inhalants. Most young users don't realize how dangerous inhalants can be. Inhalants are widely available and inexpensive, and parents should be mindful about how and where they store common household products.

Inhalants and Asthma

Asthma is a chronic disease that affects the respiratory system. Different triggers cause the airways to constrict the flow of air. An attack can become very serious and even life-threatening. Asthma is most commonly treated with drugs that are inhaled, although other drugs exist that can be taken orally. There are many different types of drugs that can be used to treat asthma and should be used depending on the situation.

Salbutamol, levalbuterol, terbutaline, and bitolterol are all short acting agents. These can be used to relieve an attack, but only are active for a short period of time. Salmeterol, formoterol, bambuterol, and albuterol are long-term acting agents, continuing to have an effect for around 12 hours. These drugs can be used to treat an attack but may need a fast acting drug to help completely control the attack.

Steroids

Anabolic steroids are a group of powerful compounds that are synthetic derivatives of the male sex hormone testosterone. These drugs are used illegally by body builders, long-distance runners, cyclists and various other athletes who claim steroids give them a competitive advantage and/or improve their physical performance. Taken in combination with a program of muscle-building exercise and diet, steroids may contribute to increases in body weight and muscular strength. Approximately 2% of teenagers will use steroids before they graduate from high school.

STEROID HEALTH HAZARDS

Irreversible side-effects. Steroid users are vulnerable to more than 70 physical and psychological side effects, many of which are irreversible. Steroid use most seriously injures the liver and cardiovascular and reproductive systems. In males, steroids can cause withered testicles, sterility, and hair loss. In females, steroids can lead to irreversible masculine traits such as breast reduction. Psychological effects in both sexes can include depression and an increase in aggressive behavior.

Long-term problems. While some side effects appear quickly, other potential health effects, such as heart attacks and strokes, may not occur for years. Steroid abuse in young adults can interfere with bone growth and lead to permanently stunted growth. People who inject steroids also risk contracting HIV and other blood-borne diseases from infected needles.

POSITIVE STEROID BENEFITS

Anabolic steroids are steroids which are focused on anabolic effects. In other words, they are mainly used to increase muscle mass, protein synthesis, and bone density. Anabolic steroids are the type of steroids that an athlete would use to increase their performance.

Narcotics

The term "narcotic," derived from the Greek word for stupor, originally referred to a variety of substances that dulled the senses and relieved pain. Today, the term is used in a number of ways. Some individuals define narcotics as those substances that bind at opiate receptors (cellular membrane proteins activated by substances like heroin or morphine) while others refer to any illicit substance as a narcotic. In a legal context, narcotic refers to opium, opium derivitives, and their semi-synthetic substitutes. Cocaine and coca leaves, which are also classified as "narcotics" in the Controlled Substances Act (CSA), neither bind opiate receptors nor produce morphine-like effects, and are discussed in the section on stimulants. For the purposes of this discussion, the term narcotic refers to drugs that produce morphine-like effects.

Narcotics are used therapeutically to treat pain, suppress cough, alleviate diarrhea, and induce anesthesia. Narcotics are administered in a variety of ways. Some are taken orally, transdermally (skin patches), or injected. They are also available in suppositories. As drugs of abuse, they are often smoked, sniffed, or injected. Drug effects depend heavily on the dose, route of administration, and previous exposure to the drug. Aside from their medical use, narcotics produce a general sense of well-being by reducing tension, anxiety, and aggression. These effects are helpful in a therapeutic setting but can tribute to their abuse.

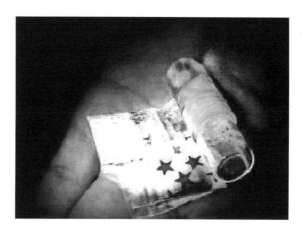

Narcotic use is associated with a variety of unwanted effects including drowsiness, inability to concentrate, apathy, lessened physical activity, constriction of the pupils, dilation of the subcutaneous blood vessels causing flushing of the face and neck, constipation, nausea and vomiting, and most significantly, respiratory depression. As the dose is increased, the subjective, analgesic (pain relief), and toxic effect become more pronounced. Except in cases of acute intoxication, there is no loss of motor coordination or slurred speech as occurs with many depressants.

Among the hazards of illicit drug use are the ever-increasing risks of infection, disease, and overdose. While pharmaceutical products have a known concentration and purity, clandestinely produced street drugs have unknown compositions. Medical complications common among narcotic abusers arise primarily from adulterants found in street drugs and in the non-sterile practices of injecting. Skin, lung, and brain abscesses, endocarditis (inflammation of the lining of the heart), hepatitis, and AIDS are commonly found among narcotic abusers. Since there is no simple way to determine the purity of a drug that is sold on the street, the effects of illicit narcotic use are unpredictable and can be fatal. Physical signs of narcotic overdose include constricted (pinpoint) pupils, cold clammy skin, confusion, convulsions, severe drowsiness, and respiratory depression (slow or troubled breathing).

With repeated use of narcotics, tolerance and dependence develop. The development of tolerance is characterized by a shortened duration and a decreased intensity of analgesia, euphoria, and sedation, which creates the need to consume progressively larger doses to attain the desired effect. Tolerance does not develop uniformly for all actions of these drugs, giving rise to a number of toxic effects. Although tolerant users can consume doses far in excess of the dose they originally took, physical dependence refers to an alteration of normal body functions that necessitates the continued presence of a drug in order to prevent a withdrawal or abstinence syndrome. The intensity and character of the physical symptoms experienced during withdrawal are directly related to the particular drug of abuse, the total daily dose, the interval between doses, the duration of use, and the health and personality of the user. In general, shorter acting narcotics tend to produce shorter, more intense withdrawal symptoms, while longer acting narcotics produce a withdrawal syndrome that is protracted but tends to be less severe. Although unpleasant, withdrawal from narcotics is rarely life threatening.

The withdrawal symptoms associated with heroin/morphine addiction are usually experienced shortly before the time of the next scheduled dose. Early symptoms include watery eyes, runny nose, yawning, and sweating. Restlessness, irritability, loss of appetite, nausea, tremors, and drug craving appear as the syndrome progresses. Severe depression and vomiting are common. The heart rate and blood pressure are elevated. Chills alternating with flushing and excessive sweating are also characteristic symptoms. Pains in the bones and muscles of the back and extremities occur, as do muscle spasms. At any point during this process, a suitable narcotic can be administered that will dramatically reverse the withdrawal symptoms. Without intervention, the syndrome will run its course, and most of the overt physical symptoms will disappear within 7 to 10 days.

The psychological dependence associated with narcotic addiction is complex and protracted. Long after the physical need for the drug has passed, the addict may continue to think and talk about the use of drugs and feel strange or overwhelmed coping with daily activities without being under the influence of drugs. There is a high probability that relapse will occur after narcotic withdrawal when neither the physical environment nor the behavioral motivators that contributed to the abuse have been altered.

There are two major patterns of narcotic abuse or dependence seen in the United States. One involves individuals whose drug use was initiated within the context of medical treatment who escalate their dose by obtaining the drug through fraudulent prescriptions and "doctor shopping" or branching out to illicit drugs. The other; more common, pattern of abuse is initiated outside the therapeutic setting with experimental or recreational use of narcotics. The majority of individuals in this category may abuse narcotics sporadically for months or even years. Although they may not become addicts, the social, medical, and legal consequences of their behavior are very serious. Some experimental users will escalate their narcotic use and will eventually become dependent, both physically and psychologically. The younger an individual is when drug use is initiated, the more likely the drug use will progress to dependence and addiction.

NARCOTICS OF NATURAL ORIGIN

The poppy papaver somniferum is the source for non-synthetic narcotics. It was grown in the Mediterranean region as early as 5000 B.C., and has since been cultivated in a number of countries throughout the world. The milky fluid that seeps from incisions in the unripe seedpod of this poppy has, since ancient times, been scraped by hand and air-dried to produce what is known as opium. A more modern method of harvesting is by the industrial poppy straw process of extracting alkaloids from the mature dried plant. The extract may be in liquid, solid, or powder form, although most poppy straw concentrate available commercially is a fine brownish powder. More than 500 tons of opium or its equivalent in poppy straw concentrate are legally imported into the United States annually for legitimate medical use.

SYNTHETIC NARCOTICS

In contrast to the pharmaceutical products derived from opium, synthetic narcotics are produced entirely within the laboratory. The continuing search for products that retain the analgesic properties of morphine without the consequent dangers of tolerance and dependence has yet to yield a product that is not susceptible to abuse. A number of clandestinely-produced drugs, as well as drugs that have accepted medical uses, fall within this category.

HEROIN

The function of heroin is similar to that of morphine. The biggest difference between the two is the speed with which they take effect, and the strength. Heroin takes effect about three times faster than morphine and is stronger. However, it is also a Schedule I drug. This means that it is highly addictive, and has no accepted medical purpose, unlike morphine.

It is estimated that around 3% of heroin users overdose per year. It may not seem like many, but it is estimated that over 3 million people have done heroin at some point in their lives. Taken as a whole, 3% of 3 million is 900,000 people. Because heroin depresses the body, consuming too much can kill a person. One way for heroin overdose to occur is actually when a person is trying to quit. If someone has not had heroin for a period of time, their tolerance lowers, like it would with alcohol. If the person then returns to the same levels they previously used, they will overdose. Another method is if a person is combining heroin with other types of substance abuse. For example, heroin depresses the body and so does alcohol. If a person mixes the two in large quantities, they will overdose. Heroin users also have an increased risk of developing hepatic disease, respiratory disease, pulmonary disease, and many other problems.

Narcan, or naloxone hydrochloride, is used to counter the effects of opiate overdose, such as with heroin or morphine. Narcan works by blocking the opiate receptors in the body. While it is sometimes distributed for emergency situations, it is increasingly used to counter addiction problems as well.

Hallucinogens

Hallucinogens are among the oldest known group of drugs used for their ability to alter human perception and mood. For centuries, many of the naturally occurring hallucinogens found in plants and fungi have been used for a variety of shamanistic practices. In more recent years, a number of synthetic hallucinogens have been produced, some of which are much more potent than their naturally occurring counterparts.

The biochemical, pharmacological, and physiological basis for hallucinogenic activity is not well understood. Even the name for this class of drugs is not ideal, since hallucinogens do not always produce hallucinations.

However, taken in non-toxic dosages, these substances produce changes in perception, thought, and mood. Physiological effects include elevated heart rate, increased blood pressure, and dilated pupils. Sensory effects include perceptual distortions that vary with dose, setting, and mood.

Synesthesia is when a person's perception of two or more senses is mixed. This phenomenon is typical of hallucinogenic drugs. For example, if a person perceives a sight as a sound or "smelling" colors.

Psychic effects include disorders of thought associated with time and space. Time may appear to stand still and forms and colors seem to change and take on new significance. This experience may be either pleasurable or extremely frightening. It should be stressed that the effects of hallucinogens are unpredictable each time they are used.

Weeks or even months after some hallucinogens have been taken, the user may experience flashbacks – fragmentary recurrences of certain aspects of the drug experience in the absence of actually taking the drug. The occurrence of a flashback is unpredictable, but is more likely to occur during times of stress and seem to occur more frequently in younger individuals. With time, these episodes diminish and become less intense.

The abuse of hallucinogens in the United States received much public attention in the 1960s and 1970s. A subsequent decline in their use in the 1980s may be attributed to real or perceived hazards associated with taking these drugs.

However, a resurgence of the use of hallucinogens is cause for concern. According to the 2003 Monitoring the Future Study, 10.6 percent of 12th graders reported hallucinogenic use in their lifetime. According to the 2003 National Survey on Drug Use and Health, approximately 1 million Americans were current hallucinogen users. Hallucinogenic mushrooms, LSD, and MDMA are popular among junior and senior high school students who use hallucinogens.

There is a considerable body of literature that links the use of some of the hallucinogenic substances to neuronal damage in animals, and recent data support that some hallucinogens are neurotoxic to humans. However, the most common danger of hallucinogen use is impaired judgment that often leads to rash decisions and accidents.

LSD

Lysergic acid diethylamide (LSD) is the most potent hallucinogen known to science, as well as the most highly studied. LSD was originally synthesized in 1938 by Dr. Albert Hoffman.

However, its hallucinogenic effects were unknown until 1943 when Hoffman accidentally consumed some LSD. It was later found that an oral dose of as little as 0.000025 grams (or 25 micrograms, equal in weight to a couple grains of salt) is capable of producing rich and vivid hallucinations. Because of its structural similarity to a chemical present in the brain and its similarity in effects to certain aspects of psychosis, LSD was used as a research tool to study mental illness. LSD abuse was popularized in the 1960s by individuals like Timothy Leary who encouraged American students to "turn on, tune in, and drop out." LSD use has varied over the years but it still remains a significant drug of abuse. In 2003, lifetime prevalence of LSD use for 8th and 12th graders was 2.1 and 5.9 percent, respectively.

The average effective oral dose is from 20 to 80 micrograms with the effects of higher doses lasting for 10 to 12 hours. LSD is usually sold in the form of impregnated paper (blotter acid), typically imprinted with colorful graphic designs. It has also been encountered in tablets (microdots), thin squares of gelatin (window panes), in sugar cubes and, rarely, in liquid form.

Physical reactions may include dilated pupils, lowered body temperature, nausea, "goose bumps," profuse perspiration, increased blood sugar, and rapid heart rate. During the first hour after ingestion, the user may experience visual changes with extreme changes in mood. In the hallucinatory state, the LSD user may suffer impaired depth and time perception, accompanied by distorted perception of the size and shape of objects, movements, color, sound, touch, and the user's own body image. During this period, the ability to perceive objects through the senses is distorted: a user may describe "hearing colors" and "seeing sounds." The ability to make sensible judgments and see common dangers is impaired, making the user susceptible to personal injury. After an LSD "trip," the user may suffer acute anxiety or depression for a variable period of time. Flashbacks have been reported days or even months after taking the last dose.

PSILOCYBIN, PSILOCYN AND OTHER TRYPTAMINES

A number of Schedule I hallucinogenic substances are classified chemically as tryptamines. Most of these are found in nature but many, if not all, can be produced synthetically. Psilocybin and psilocyn (4-hydroxy-N,N-dimethyltryptamine) are obtained from certain mushrooms indigenous to tropical and subtropical regions of South America, Mexico, and the United States. As pure chemicals at doses of 10 to 20 mg, these hallucinogens produce muscle relaxation, dilation of pupils, vivid visual and auditory distortions, and emotional disturbances. However, the effects produced by consuming preparations of dried or brewed mushrooms are far less predictable and largely depend on the particular mushrooms used and the age and preservation of the extract. There are many species of "magic" mushrooms that contain varying amounts of these tryptamines, as well as uncertain amounts of other chemicals. As a consequence, the hallucinogenic activity and the extent of toxicity produced by various plant samples are often unknown.

Diethyltryptamine (DMT) N,N-Dimethyltryptamine has a long history of use and is found in a variety of plants and seeds. It can also be produced synthetically. It is ineffective when taken orally, unless combined with another drug that inhibits its metabolism. Generally it is sniffed, smoked, or injected. The effective hallucinogenic dose in humans is about 50 to 100 mg and lasts for about 45 to 60 minutes. Because the effects last only about an hour, the experience has been referred to as a "businessman's trip."

A number of other hallucinogens have very similar structures and properties to those of DMT. Diethyltryptamine (DET) N,N-Diethyltryptamine, for example, is an analogue of DMT and produces the same pharmacological effects but is somewhat less potent than DMT. Alpha-ethyltryptamine (AET) is another tryptamine hallucinogen added to the list of Schedule I hallucinogens in 1994. Bufotenine (5-hydroxy-N,N-dimethyl-tryptamine) is a Schedule I substance found in certain mushrooms, seeds, and skin glands of Bufo toads. In general, most bufotenine preparations from natural sources are extremely toxic. N,N-Diisopropyl-5-methoxytryptamine (referred to as Foxy-Methoxy) is an orally active tryptamine recently encountered in the United States.

PEYOTE & MESCALINE

Peyote is a small, spineless cactus, Lophophora williamsii, whose principal active ingredient is the hallucinogen mescaline (3, 4, 5-trimethoxyphenethylamine). From earliest recorded time, peyote has been used by natives in northern Mexico and the southwestern United States as a part of their religious rites.

The top of the cactus above ground – also referred to as the crown – consists of disc-shaped buttons that are cut from the roots and dried. These buttons are generally chewed or soaked in water to produce an intoxicating liquid. The hallucinogenic dose of mescaline is about 0.3 to 0.5 grams and lasts about 12 hours. While peyote produced rich visual hallucinations that were important to the native American peyote users, the full spectrum of effects served as a chemically induced model of mental illness. Mescaline can be extracted from peyote or produced synthetically. Both peyote and mescaline are listed in the CSA as Schedule I hallucinogens.

Many chemical variations of mescaline and amphetamine have been synthesized for their "feel good" effects. 4-Methyl-2, 5-dimethoxyamphetamine (DOM) was introduced into the San Francisco drug scene in the late 1960s and was nicknamed STP; an acronym for "Serenity, Tranquility, and Peace." Other illicitly produced analogues include 4-bromo-2, 5-dimethoxyamphetamine (DOB) and 4-bromo-2, 5-dimethoxy-phenethylamine (2C-B or Nexus). In 2000, *para*-methoxyamphetamine (PMA,) and *para*-methoxymethamphetamine (PMMA) were identified in tablets sold as Ecstasy. PMA, which first appeared on the illicit market briefly in the early 1970s, is associated with a number of deaths in both the United States and Europe.

NEW HALLUCINOGENS

A number of phenethylamine and tryptamine analogues have been encountered on the illicit market. Those recently placed under federal control include 2C-T-7 (dimethoxy-4-(n)-propylthiophenethylamine), permanently placed in Schedule I in March 2004, and 5-MeO-DIPT (5-methoxy-diisopropyltryptamine) and AMT (alpha-methyltryptamine), which were placed in Schedule I on an emergency basis in April

2003. In addition, a number of other analogues are being encountered. These include DIPT (N,N-diisopropyltryptamine), DPT (N,N-dipropyltryptamine), 5-MeO-AMT (5-methoxy-alpha-methyltryptamine), MIPT (N, N-methylisopropyltryptamine) and 5-MeO-MIPT (5-Methoxy, N,N-methylisopropyltryptamine) to name a few. While these drugs are not specifically listed under the CSA, individuals trafficking in these substances can be prosecuted under the Analogue Statute of the CSA. The ever-increasing number of these types of hallucinogens being encountered by law enforcement is a testament to the efforts of individuals to engage in profitable drug enterprises while trying to avoid criminal prosecution.

MDMA (ECSTASY) AND OTHER PHENETHYLAMINES

Methylenedioxymethamphetamine (MDMA, Ecstasy) was first synthesized in 1912 but remained in relative obscurity for many years. In the 1980s, MDMA gained popularity as a drug of abuse resulting in its final placement in Schedule I of the CSA. Today, MDMA is extremely popular. In 2000, it was estimated that two million tablets were smuggled into the United States every week.

MDMA produces both amphetamine-like stimulation and mild mescaline-like hallucinations. It is touted as a "feel good" drug with an undeserved reputation of safety. MDMA produces euphoria, increased energy, increased sensual arousal, and enhanced tactile sensations. However, it also produces nerve cell damage that can result in psychiatric disturbances and long-term cognitive impairments. The user will often experience increased muscle tension, tremors, blurred vision, and hyperthermia. The increased body temperature can result in organ failure and death.

MDMA is usually distributed in tablet form and taken orally at doses ranging from 50 to 200 mg. Individual tablets are often imprinted with graphic designs or commercial logos, and typically contain 80-100 mg of MDMA. After oral administration, effects are felt within 30 to 45 minutes, peak at 60 to 90 minutes, and last for 4 to 6 hours. Analysis of seized MDMA tablets indicates that about 80 percent of all samples actually contain MDMA. About 10 percent of the MDMA-positive samples also contain MDA (3, 4-methylenedioxyamphetamine) and MDEA (3, 4-methylenedioxyethylamphetamine), while another 10 percent contain amphetamine, methamphetamine, or both. Fraudulent MDMA tablets frequently contain combinations of ephedrine, dextromethorphan, and caffeine or newer piperazine compounds.

Hundreds of compounds can be produced by making slight modifications to the phenethylamine molecule. Some of these analogues are pharmacologically active and differ from one another in potency, speed of onset, duration of action, and capacity to modify mood, with or without producing overt hallucinations. The drugs are usually taken orally, sometimes snorted, and rarely injected. Because they are produced in clandestine laboratories, they are seldom pure and the amount in a capsule or tablet is likely to vary considerably.

According to the National Survey on Drug Use and Health, initiation of Ecstasy use has increased from 1993 until 2001, when it peaked at 1.8 million new users. In 2002 the number declined to 1.1 million. Two-thirds (66 percent) of new Ecstasy users in 2002 were 18 or older, and 50 percent were male.

PHENCYCLIDINE AND RELATED DRUGS

In the 1950s, phencyclidine (PCP) was investigated as an anesthetic but, due to the side effects of confusion and delirium, its development for human use was discontinued. It became commercially available for use as a veterinary anesthetic in the 1960s under the trade name of Sernylan® and was placed in Schedule III of the CSA. In 1978, due to considerable abuse, phencyclidine was transferred to Schedule II of the CSA and manufacturing of Sernylan® was discontinued. Today, virtually all of the phencyclidine encountered on the illicit market in the United States is produced in clandestine laboratories.

PCP is illicitly marketed under a number of other names, including Angel Dust, Supergrass, Killer Weed, Embalming Fluid, and Rocket Fuel, reflecting the range of its bizarre and volatile effects. In its pure form, it is a white crystalline powder that readily dissolves in water. However, most PCP on the illicit market contains a number of contaminants as a result of makeshift manufacturing, causing the color to range from tan to brown, and the consistency from powder to a gummy mass. Although sold in tablets and capsules as well as in powder and liquid form, it is commonly applied to a leafy material, such as parsley, mint, oregano, or marijuana, and smoked.

The drug's effects are as varied as its appearance. A moderate amount of PCP often causes the user to feel detached, distant, and estranged from his surroundings. Numbness, slurred speech, and loss of coordination may be accompanied by a sense of strength and invulnerability. A blank stare, rapid and involuntary eye movements, and an exaggerated gait are among the more observable effects. Auditory hallucinations, image distortion, severe mood disorders, and amnesia may also occur. In some users, PCP may cause acute anxiety and a feeling of impending doom; in others, paranoia and violent hostility; and in some, it may produce a psychosis indistinguishable from schizophrenia. PCP use is associated with a number of risks, and many believe it to be one of the most dangerous drugs of abuse.

Modification of the manufacturing process may yield chemically related analogues capable of producing psychic effects similar to PCP. Four of these substances, N-ethyl-l-phenylcyclohexylamine or PCE, 1-(phenylcyclohexyl)pyrrolidine or PCPy, l-[l-(2-thienyl)cyclohexyl]piperdine or TCP, and l-[l-(2-thienyl)cyclohexyl]pyrrolidine or TCPy have been encountered on the illicit market and have been placed in Schedule I of the CSA. Telazol®, a Schedule III veterinary anesthetic containing tiletamine (a PCP analogue), in combination with zolazepam, (a benzodiazepine), is sporadically encountered as a drug of abuse.

KETAMINE

Ketamine is a rapidly acting general anesthetic. Its pharmacological profile is essentially the same as phencyclidine. Like PCP, ketamine is referred to as a dissociative anesthetic because patients feel detached or disconnected from their pain and environment when anesthetized with this drug. Unlike most anesthetics, ketamine produces only mild respiratory depression and appears to stimulate, not depress, the cardiovascular system. In addition, ketamine has both analgesic and amnesic properties and is associated with less confusion, irrationality, and violent behavior than PCP. Use of ketamine as a general anesthetic for humans has been limited due to adverse effects including delirium and hallucinations. Today, it is primarily used in veterinary medicine, but has some utility for emergency surgery in humans.

Although ketamine has been marketed in the United States for many years, it was only recently associated with significant diversion and abuse and placed in Schedule III of the CSA in 1999. Known in the drug culture as "Special K" or "Super K," ketamine has become a staple at dance parties or "raves." Ketamine is supplied to the illicit market by the diversion of legitimate pharmaceuticals (Ketaset®, Ketalar®). It is usually distributed as a powder obtained by removing the liquid from the pharmaceutical products. As a drug of abuse, ketamine can be administered orally, snorted, or injected. It is also sprinkled on marijuana or tobacco and smoked. After oral or intranasal administration, effects are evident in about 10 to 15 minutes and are over in about an hour.

After intravenous use, effects begin almost immediately and reach peak effects within minutes. Ketamine can act as a depressant or a psychedelic. Low doses produce vertigo, ataxia, slurred speech, slow reaction time, and euphoria. Intermediate doses produce disorganized thinking, altered body image, and a feeling of unreality with vivid visual hallucinations. High doses produce analgesia, amnesia, and coma.

 *Psychoactive Drugs*

Psychoactive drugs are drugs which directly affect the brain. This means that they affect mood, thought process, and behavior. Common examples of psychoactive drugs are alcohol, heroin, cocaine, LSD, and caffeine. Psychoactive drugs are grouped in three basic categories. Depressants slow down the nervous system, like heroin. Stimulants speed up the nervous system, such as caffeine. Hallucinogens alter a person's perception of reality, such as LSD.

Thalidomide

Thalidomide was once used as a drug to help women with morning sickness. However as time went on, doctors began to notice an increase in the amount of birth defects, which was eventually linked to thalidomide. Women who take thalidomide during their first trimester are more likely to have children with deformed limbs. Thalidomide was widely distributed in the 1950's, and by the time it was taken off the market in the late 1960's over 10,000 children are believed to have been effected by it.

Controlled Substances Act

FORMAL SCHEDULING

The Controlled Substances Act (CSA) was passed by Congress as Title II of the Comprehensive Drug Abuse Prevention and Control Act of 1970. The CSA stated that there were to be five schedules of drugs, based on their medical uses and potential for abuse. The Drug Enforcement Administration (DEA) and Food and Drug Administration (FDA) decide which drugs are in which category.

The Controlled Substances Act (CSA) places all substances that were in some manner regulated under existing federal law into one of five schedules. This placement is based upon the substance's medical use, potential for abuse, and safety or dependence liability. The Act also provides a mechanism for substances to be controlled, or added to a schedule; decontrolled, or removed from control; and rescheduled or transferred from one schedule to another. The procedure for these actions is found in Section 201 of the Act (21 U.S.C. 811).

Proceedings to add, delete, or change the schedule of a drug or other substance may be initiated by the Drug Enforcement Administration (DEA), the Department of Health and Human Services (HHS), or by petition from any interested person: the manufacturer of a drug, a medical society or association, a pharmacy association, a public interest group concerned with drug abuse, a state or local government agency, or an individual citizen. When a petition is received by the DEA, the agency begins its own investigation of the drug.

The DEA also may begin an investigation of a drug at any time based upon information received from law enforcement laboratories, state and local law enforcement and regulatory agencies, or other sources of information.

Once the DEA has collected the necessary data, the DEA Administrator, by authority of the Attorney General, requests from HHS a scientific and medical evaluation and recommendation as to whether the drug or other substance should be controlled or removed from control. This request is sent to the Assistant Secretary of Health of HHS. HHS solicits information from the Commissioner of the Food and Drug Administration (FDA), evaluations and recommendations from the National Institute on Drug Abuse, and on occasion from the scientific and medical community at large. The Assistant Secretary, by authority of the Secretary, compiles the information and transmits back to the DEA a medical and scientific evaluation regarding the drug or other substance, a recommendation as to whether the drug should be controlled, and in what schedule it should be placed.

The medical and scientific evaluations are binding in the DEA with respect to scientific and medical matters and form a part of the scheduling decision. The recommendation on the initial scheduling of a substance is binding only to the extent that if HHS recommends that the substance not be controlled, the DEA may not add it to the schedules.

Once the DEA has received the scientific and medical evaluation from HHS, the Administrator will evaluate all available data and make a final decision whether to propose that a drug or other substance should be removed or controlled and into which schedule it should be placed.

The threshold issue is whether the drug or other substance has potential for abuse. If a drug does not have a potential for abuse, it cannot be controlled. Although the term "potential for abuse" is not defined in the CSA, there is much discussion of the term in the legislative history of the Act. The following items are indicators that a drug or other substance has a potential for abuse:

1. There is evidence that individuals are taking the drug or other substance in amounts sufficient to create a hazard to their health or to the safety of other individuals or to the community; or

2. There is significant diversion of the drug or other substance from legitimate drug channels; or

3. Individuals are taking the drug or other substance on their own initiative rather than on the basis of medical advice from a practitioner licensed by law to administer such drugs; or

4. The drug is a new drug so related in its action to a drug or other substance already listed as having a potential for abuse to make it likely that the drug will have the same potential for abuse as such drugs, thus making it reasonable to assume that there may be significant diversions from legitimate channels, significant use contrary to or without medical advice, or that it has a substantial

capability of creating hazards to the health of the user or to the safety of the community. Of course, evidence of actual abuse of a substance is indicative that a drug has a potential for abuse.

In determining into which schedule a drug or other substance should be placed, or whether a substance should be decontrolled or rescheduled, certain factors are required to be considered. Specific findings are not required for each factor. These factors are listed in Section 201 of the CSA as follows:

1. **The drug's actual or relative potential for abuse.**

2. **Scientific evidence of the drug's pharmacological effects.** The state of knowledge with respect to the effects of a specific drug is, of course, a major consideration. For example, it is vital to know whether or not a drug has a hallucinogenic effect if it is to be controlled due to that effect. The best available knowledge of the pharmacological properties of a drug should be considered.

3. **The state of current scientific knowledge regarding the substance.** Criteria (2) and (3) are closely related. However, (2) is primarily concerned with pharmacological effects and (3) deals with all scientific knowledge with respect to the substance.

4. **Its history and current pattern of abuse.** To determine whether or not a drug should be controlled, it is important to know the pattern of abuse of that substance, including the socio-economic characteristics of the segments of the population involved in such abuse.

5. **The scope, duration, and significance of abuse.** In evaluating existing abuse, the DEA Administrator must know not only the pattern of abuse, but whether the abuse is widespread. In reaching a decision, the Administrator should consider the economics of regulation and enforcement attendant to such a decision. In addition, the Administrator should be aware of the social significance and impact of such a decision upon those people, especially the young, that would be affected by it.

6. **What, if any, risk there is to the public health.** If a drug creates dangers to the public health, in addition to or because of its abuse potential, then these dangers must also be considered by the Administrator.

7. **The drug's psychic or physiological dependence liability.** There must be an assessment of the extent to which a drug is physically addictive or psychologically habit forming, if such information is known.

8. **Whether the substance is an immediate precursor of a substance already controlled.** The CSA allows inclusion of immediate precursors on this basis

alone into the appropriate schedule and thus safeguards against possibilities of clandestine manufacture.

After considering the above listed factors, the Administrator must make specific findings concerning the drug or other substance. This will determine into which schedule the drug or other substance will be placed. These schedules are established by the CSA. They are as follows:

SCHEDULE I

- The drug or other substance has a high potential for abuse.
- The drug or other substance has no currently accepted medical use in treatment in the United States.
- There is a lack of accepted safety for use of the drug or other substance under medical supervision.
- Examples of Schedule I substances include heroin, lysergic acid diethylamide (LSD), marijuana, and methaqualone.

SCHEDULE II

- The drug or other substance has a high potential for abuse.
- The drug or other substance has a currently accepted medical use in treatment in the United States or a currently accepted medical use with severe restrictions.
- Abuse of the drug or other substance may lead to severe psychological or physical dependence.
- Examples of Schedule II substances include morphine, phencyclidine (PCP), cocaine, methadone, and methamphetamine.

SCHEDULE III

- The drug or other substance has less potential for abuse than the drugs or other substances in schedules I and II.
- The drug or other substance has a currently accepted medical use in treatment in the United States.
- Abuse of the drug or other substance may lead to moderate or low physical dependence or high psychological dependence.
- Anabolic steroids, codeine and hydrocodone with aspirin or Tylenol®, and some barbiturates are examples of Schedule III substances.

SCHEDULE IV

- The drug or other substance has a low potential for abuse relative to the drugs or other substances in Schedule III.
- The drug or other substance has a currently accepted medical use in treatment in the United States.

- Abuse of the drug or other substance may lead to limited physical dependence or psychological dependence relative to the drugs or other substances in Schedule III.
- Examples of drugs included in schedule IV are Darvon®, Talwin®, Equanil®, Valium®, and Xanax®.

SCHEDULE V

- The drug or other substance has a low potential for abuse relative to the drugs or other substances in Schedule IV.
- The drug or other substance has a currently accepted medical use in treatment in the United States.
- Abuse of the drug or other substances may lead to limited physical dependence or psychological dependence relative to the drugs or other substances in Schedule IV.
- Cough medicines with codeine are examples of Schedule V drugs.

When the DEA Administrator has determined that a drug or other substance should be controlled, decontrolled, or rescheduled, a proposal to take action is published in the *Federal Register*. The proposal invites all interested persons to file comments with the DEA. Affected parties may also request a hearing with the DEA. If no hearing is requested, the DEA will evaluate all comments received and publish a final order in the *Federal Register*, controlling the drug as proposed or with modifications based upon the written comments filed. This order will set the effective dates for imposing the various requirements of the CSA.

If a hearing is requested, the DEA will enter into discussions with the party or parties requesting a hearing in an attempt to narrow the issue for litigation. If necessary, a hearing will then be held before an Administrative Law Judge. The judge will take evidence on factual issues and hear arguments on legal questions regarding the control of the drug. Depending on the scope and complexity of the issues, the hearing may be brief or quite extensive. The Administrative Law Judge, at the close of the hearing, prepares findings of fact and conclusions of law and a recommended decision, which is submitted to the DEA Administrator. The DEA Administrator will review these documents, as well as the underlying material, and prepare his/her own findings of fact and conclusions of law (which may or may not be the same as those drafted by the Administrative Law Judge). The DEA Administrator then publishes a final order in the *Federal Register* either scheduling the drug or other substance or declining to do so.

Once the final order is published in the *Federal Register*, interested parties have 30 days to appeal to a U.S. Court of Appeals to challenge the order. Findings of fact by the Administrator are deemed conclusive if supported by "substantial evidence." The order imposing controls is not stayed during the appeal, however, unless so ordered by the Court.

EMERGENCY OR TEMPORARY SCHEDULING

The CSA was amended by the Comprehensive Crime Control Act of 1984. This Act included a provision which allows the DEA Administrator to place a substance, on a temporary basis, into Schedule I when necessary to avoid an imminent hazard to the public safety.

This emergency scheduling authority permits the scheduling of a substance which is not currently controlled, is being abused, and is a risk to the public health while the formal rule-making procedures described in the CSA are being conducted. This emergency scheduling applies only to substances with no accepted medical use. A temporary scheduling order may be issued for one year with a possible extension of up to six months if formal scheduling procedures have been initiated. The proposal and order are published in the *Federal Register* as are the proposals and orders for formal scheduling.

CONTROLLED SUBSTANCE ANALOGUES

A new class of substances was created by the Anti-Drug Abuse Act of 1986. Controlled substance analogues are substances that are not controlled substances, but may be found in the illicit traffic. They are structurally or pharmacologically similar to Schedule I or II controlled substances and have no legitimate medical use. A substance which meets the definition of a controlled substance analogue and is intended for human consumption is treated under the CSA as if it were a controlled substance in Schedule I.

INTERNATIONAL TREATY OBLIGATIONS

United States treaty obligations may require that a drug or other substance be controlled under the CSA, or rescheduled if existing controls are less stringent than those required by a treaty. The procedures for these scheduling actions are found in Section 201(d) of the Act.

The United States is a party to the Single Convention on Narcotic Drugs of 1961, designed to establish effective control over international and domestic traffic in narcotics, coca leaf, cocaine, and cannabis. A second treaty, the Convention on Psychotropic Substances of 1971, which entered into force in 1976, is designed to establish comparable control over stimulants, depressants, and hallucinogens. Congress ratified this treaty in 1980.

Regulation

The CSA creates a closed system of distribution for those authorized to handle controlled substances. The cornerstone of this system is the registration of all those authorized by DEA to handle controlled substances. All individuals and firms that are registered are required to maintain complete and accurate inventories and records of all transactions involving controlled substances, as well as security for the storage of controlled substances.

REGISTRATION

Any person who handles or intends to handle controlled substances must obtain a registration issued by DEA. A unique number is assigned to each legitimate handler of controlled drugs: importer, exporter, manufacturer, distributor, hospital, pharmacy, practitioner, and researcher. This number must be made available to the supplier by the customer prior to the purchase of a controlled substance. Thus, the opportunity for unauthorized transactions is greatly diminished.

RECORD KEEPING

The CSA requires that complete and accurate records be kept of all quantities of controlled substances manufactured, purchased, and sold. Each substance must be inventoried every two years. Some limited exceptions to the record-keeping requirements may apply to certain categories of registrants.

From these records it is possible to trace the flow of any drug from the time it is first imported or manufactured, through the distribution level, to the pharmacy or hospital that dispensed it, and then to the actual patient who received the drug. The mere existence of this requirement is sufficient to discourage many forms of diversion. It actually serves large drug corporations as an internal check to uncover diversion, such as pilferage by employees.

There is one distinction between scheduled items for record keeping requirements. Records for Schedule I and II drugs must be kept separate from all other records of the handler; records for Schedule III, IV, and V substances must be kept in a "readily retrievable" form. The former method allows for more expeditious investigations involving the highly abusable substances in Schedules I and II.

DISTRIBUTION

The keeping of records is required for distribution of a controlled substance from one manufacturer to another, from manufacturer to distributor, and from distributor to dispenser. In the case of Schedule I and II drugs, the supplier must have a special order form from the customer. This order form (DEA Form 222) is issued by DEA only to persons who are properly registered to handle Schedules I and II. The form is pre-printed with the name and address of the customer. The drugs must be shipped to this name and address. The use of this device is a special reinforcement of the registration requirement; it ensures that only authorized individuals may obtain Schedule I and II drugs. Another benefit of the form is the special monitoring it permits. The form is issued in triplicate: the customer keeps one copy; two copies go to the supplier who, after filling the order, keeps a copy and forwards the third copy to the nearest DEA office.

For drugs in Schedules III, IV, and V, no order form is necessary. The supplier in each case, however, is under an obligation to verify the authenticity of the customer. The supplier is held fully accountable for any drugs that are shipped to a purchaser who does not have a valid registration. Manufacturers must submit periodic reports of the Schedule I and II controlled substances they produce in bulk and dosage forms. They also report the manufactured quantity and form of each narcotic substance listed in Schedules III, IV, and V, as well as the quantity of synthesized psychotropic substances listed in Schedules I, II, III, and IV.

Distributors of controlled substances must report the quantity and form of all their transactions of controlled drugs listed in Schedules I and II and narcotics listed in Schedule III. Both manufacturers and distributors are required to provide reports of their annual inventories of these controlled substances. This data is entered into a system called the Automated Reports and Consolidated Orders System (ARCOS). It enables the DEA to monitor the distribution of controlled substances throughout the country, and to identify retail level registrants that receive unusual quantities of controlled substances.

DISPENSING TO PATIENTS

The dispensing of a controlled substance is the delivery of the controlled substance to the ultimate user, who may be a patient or research subject. Special control mechanisms operate here as well. Schedule I drugs are those which have no currently accepted medical use in the United States; they may, therefore, be used in the United States only in research situations. They generally are supplied by only a limited number of firms to properly registered and qualified researchers. Controlled substances may be dispensed by a practitioner by direct administration, by prescription, or by dispensing from office supplies.

Records must be maintained by the practitioner of all dispensing of controlled substances from office supplies and of certain administrations. The CSA does not require the practitioner to maintain copies of prescriptions, but certain states require the use of multiple-copy prescriptions for Schedule II and other specified controlled substances.

The determination to place drugs on prescription is within the jurisdiction of the FDA. Unlike other prescription drugs, however, controlled substances are subject to additional restrictions. Schedule II prescription orders must be written and signed by the practitioner; they may not be telephoned into the pharmacy except in an emergency. In addition, a prescription for a Schedule II drug may not be refilled; the patient must see the practitioner again in order to obtain more drugs. For Schedule III and IV drugs, the prescription order may be either written or oral (that is, by telephone to the pharmacy). In addition, the patient may (if authorized by the practitioner) have the prescription refilled up to five times and at anytime within six months from the date the prescription was issued.

Schedule V includes some prescription drugs and many narcotic preparations, including antitussives and antidiarrheals. Even here, however, the law imposes restrictions beyond those normally required for the over-the-counter sales; for example, the patient must be at least 18 years of age, must offer some form of identification, and have his or her name entered into a special log maintained by the pharmacist as part of a special record.

QUOTAS

DEA limits the quantity of Schedule I and II controlled substances that may be produced in the United States in any given calendar year. By utilizing available data on sales and inventories of these controlled substances, and taking into account estimates of drug usage provided by the FDA, the DEA establishes annual aggregate production quotas for Schedule I and II controlled substances. The aggregate production quota is allocated among the various manufacturers who are registered to manufacture the specific drug. DEA also allocates the amount of bulk drug which may be procured by those companies that prepare the drug into dosage units.

SECURITY

DEA registrants are required by regulation to maintain certain security for the storage and distribution of controlled substances. Manufacturers and distributors of Schedule I and II substances must store controlled substances in specially constructed vaults or highly rated safes, and maintain electronic security for all storage areas. Lesser physical security requirements apply to retail level registrants such as hospitals and pharmacies. All registrants are required to make every effort to ensure that controlled substances in their possession are not diverted into the illicit market. This requires operational as well as physical security. For example, registrants are responsible for ensuring that controlled substances are distributed only to other registrants that are authorized to receive them, or to legitimate patients and consumers.

Penalties

The CSA provides penalties for unlawful manufacturing, distribution, and dispensing of controlled substances. The penalties are basically determined by the schedule of the drug or other substance, and sometimes are specified by drug name, as in the case of marijuana. As the statute has been amended since its initial passage in 1970, the penalties have been altered by Congress. The following charts are an overview of the penalties for trafficking or unlawful distribution of controlled substances. This is not inclusive of the penalties provided under the CSA.

USER ACCOUNTABILITY/PERSONAL USE PENALTIES

On November 19, 1988, Congress passed the Anti-Drug Abuse Act of 1988, P. L. 100-690. Two sections of this Act represent the U.S. Government's attempt to reduce drug abuse by dealing not just with the person who sells the illegal drug, but also with the person who buys it. The first new section is titled "User Accountability" and is codified at 21 U.S.C. § 862 and various sections of Title 42, U.S.C. The second involves "personal use amounts" of illegal drugs, and is codified at 21 U.S.C. § 844a.

USER ACCOUNTABILITY

The purpose of User Accountability is to not only make the public aware of the Federal Government's position on drug abuse, but to describe new programs intended to decrease drug abuse by holding drug abusers personally responsible for their illegal activities, and imposing civil penalties on those who violate drug laws.

It is important to remember that these penalties are in addition to the criminal penalties drug abusers are already given, and do not replace those criminal penalties.

The new User Accountability programs call for more instruction in schools, kindergarten through senior high, to educate children on the dangers of drug abuse. These programs will include participation by students, parents, teachers, local businesses and the local, state and Federal Government.

User Accountability also targets businesses interested in doing business with the Federal Government. This program requires those businesses to maintain a drug-free workplace, principally through educating employees on the dangers of drug abuse, and by informing employees of the penalties they face if they engage in illegal drug activity on company property.

There is also a provision in the law that makes public housing projects drug-free by evicting those residents who allow their units to be used for illegal drug activity, and denies federal benefits, such as housing assistance and student loans, to individuals convicted of illegal drug activity. Depending on the offense, an individual may be prohibited from ever receiving any benefit provided by the Federal Government.

PERSONAL USE AMOUNTS

This section of the 1988 Act allows the government to punish minor drug offenders without giving the offender a criminal record if the offender is in possession of only a small amount of drugs. This law is designed to impact the "user" of illicit drugs, while simultaneously saving the government the costs of a full-blown criminal investigation.

Under this section, the government has the option of imposing only a civil fine on individuals possessing only a small quantity of an illegal drug. Possession of this small quantity, identified as a "personal use amount" carries a civil fine of up to $10,000.

In determining the amount of the fine in a particular case, the drug offender's income and assets will be considered. This is accomplished through an administrative proceeding rather than a criminal trial, thus reducing the exposure of the offender to the entire criminal justice system, and reducing the costs to the offender and the government.

The value of this section is that it allows the government to punish a minor drug offender, gives the drug offender the opportunity to fully redeem himself or herself, and have all public record of the proceeding destroyed. If this was the drug offender's first offense, and the offender has paid all fines, can pass a drug test, and has not been convicted of a crime after three years, the offender can request that all proceedings be dismissed.

If the proceeding is dismissed, the drug offender can lawfully say he or she had never been prosecuted, either criminally or civilly, for a drug offense.

Congress has imposed two limitations on this section's use. It may not be used if (1) the drug offender has been previously convicted of a Federal or state drug offense; or (2) the offender has already been fined twice under this section.

Detoxification and Detection

Detoxification is the process through which the body rids itself of harmful toxins, and takes place in three basic stages. Cleansing is the first stage. In this stage the body rids itself of harmful toxins. The second stage consists of the removal cells which were killed by the toxin. The final stage is rebuilding tissue from the damage of the toxin.

Hepatic enzymes are enzymes in the liver. Higher levels of these enzymes indicate liver damage, which is often a result of substance abuse. Because of this the more hepatic enzymes a person has in their system, the more likely it is that they are doing drugs.

Treatment

Drug addiction is a treatable disorder. Through treatment that is tailored to individual needs, patients can learn to control their condition and live normal, productive lives. Like people with diabetes or heart disease, people in treatment for drug addiction learn behavioral changes and often take medications as part of their treatment regimen.

Behavioral therapies can include counseling, psychotherapy, support groups, or family therapy. Treatment medications offer help in suppressing the withdrawal syndrome and drug craving and in blocking the effects of drugs. In addition, studies show that treatment for heroin addiction using methadone at an adequate dosage level combined with behavioral therapy reduces death rates and many health problems associated with heroin abuse.

In general, the more treatment given, the better the results. Many patients require other services as well, such as medical and mental health services and HIV prevention services. Patients who stay in treatment longer than 3 months usually have better outcomes than those who stay less time. Patients who go through medically assisted withdrawal to minimize discomfort but do not receive any further treatment, perform about the same in terms of their drug use as those who were never treated. Over the last 25 years, studies have shown that treatment works to reduce drug intake and crimes committed by drug-dependent people. Researchers also have found that drug abusers who have been through treatment are more likely to have jobs.

TYPES OF TREATMENT PROGRAMS

The ultimate goal of all drug abuse treatment is to enable the patient to achieve lasting abstinence, but the immediate goals are to reduce drug use, improve the patient's ability to function, and minimize the medical and social complications of drug abuse.

There are several types of drug abuse treatment programs. Short-term methods last less than 6 months and include residential therapy, medication therapy, and drug-free outpatient therapy. Longer term treatment may include, for example, methadone maintenance outpatient treatment for opiate addicts and residential therapeutic community treatment.

In maintenance treatment for heroin addicts, people in treatment are given an oral dose of a synthetic opiate, usually methadone hydrochloride or levo-alpha-acetyl methadol (LAAM), administered at a dosage sufficient to block the effects of heroin and yield a stable, noneuphoric state free from physiological craving for opiates. In this stable state, the patient is able to disengage from drug-seeking and related criminal behavior and, with appropriate counseling and social services, become a productive member of his or her community.

Outpatient drug-free treatment does not include medications and encompasses a wide variety of programs for patients who visit a clinic at regular intervals. Most of the programs involve individual or group counseling. Patients entering these programs are abusers of drugs other than opiates or are opiate abusers for whom maintenance therapy is not recommended, such as those who have stable, well-integrated lives and only brief histories of drug dependence.

Therapeutic communities (TCs) are highly structured programs in which patients stay at a residence, typically for 6 to 12 months. Patients in TCs include those with relatively long histories of drug dependence, involvement in serious criminal activities, and seriously impaired social functioning. The focus of the TC is on the resocialization of the patient to a drug-free, crime-free lifestyle.

Short-term residential programs, often referred to as chemical dependency units, are often based on the "Minnesota Model" of treatment for alcoholism. These programs involve a 3- to 6-week inpatient treatment phase followed by extended outpatient therapy or participation in 12-step self-help groups, such as Narcotics Anonymous or Cocaine Anonymous. Chemical dependency programs for drug abuse arose in the private sector in the mid-1980s with insured alcohol/cocaine abusers as their primary patients. Today, as private provider benefits decline, more programs are extending their services to publicly funded patients.

Methadone maintenance programs are usually more successful at retaining clients with opiate dependence than are therapeutic communities, which in turn are more successful than outpatient programs that provide psychotherapy and counseling. Within various methadone programs, those that provide higher doses of methadone (usually a minimum of 60 mg.) have better retention rates. Also, those that provide other services, such as counseling, therapy, and medical care, along with methadone generally get better results than the programs that provide minimal services.

Drug treatment programs in prisons can succeed in preventing patients' return to criminal behavior, particularly if they are linked to community-based programs that continue treatment when the client leaves prison. Some of the more successful programs have reduced the rearrest rate by one-fourth to one-half. For example, the "Delaware Model," an ongoing study of comprehensive treatment of drug-addicted prison inmates, shows that prison-based treatment including a therapeutic community setting, a work release therapeutic community, and community-based aftercare reduces the probability of rearrest by 57 percent and reduces the likelihood of returning to drug use by 37 percent.

Drug abuse has a great economic impact on society-an estimated $67 billion per year. This figure includes costs related to crime, medical care, drug abuse treatment, social welfare programs, and time lost from work. Treatment of drug abuse can reduce those costs. Studies have shown that from $4 to $7 are saved for every dollar spent on treatment. It costs approximately $3,600 per month to leave a drug abuser untreated in the community, and incarceration costs approximately $3,300 per month. In contrast, methadone maintenance therapy costs about $290 per month.

For information on hotlines or counseling services, please call the Center for Substance Abuse Treatment's National Drug and Alcohol Treatment Service at 1-800-662-4357.

 Research Methods

Experimental Research
The experimental method of research is a scientific method. This is when a variable and a constant are used to test theories. A **variable** is some changing part of the person that is being studied. Age and gender are variables. A constant is the opposite of a variable.

A **constant** is a factor that always stays the same. In an experiment there is an independent variable and a dependent variable. A **dependent variable** is the variable that the experiment is trying to test or gather information about. An **independent variable** is a variable that the experimenter controls. When an experimenter uses independent and dependent variables, they are exploring the if-then relationship. Here is an example: **If** you eat a pizza a day (independent variable) **then** you will gain weight (dependent variable). The more precise the hypothesis, the more accurately you can measure the link between the two variables.

Clinical Research
Clinical research is research done with a control group and a treatment group. A good example of this is when studying a diet pill. A clinical research trial will have two groups of people who all think they are taking this drug to help them lose weight. They are all monitored and report their progress and symptoms to researchers. One group,

the control group, is not given the drug. Those persons thinking they are on the drug may still lose weight because of their positive thinking or other thoughts or outside influences. Sometimes a study is called a blind or double blind study. In a blind trial, the patients do not know they are taking the placebo. In a double blind study, neither the patient nor the doctor knows who is taking the real medicine and who is taking the placebo. This helps maintain the highest accuracy.

Correlational Research
Correlational research is used to find the amount that one variable changes in relation to another. For example, is there a correlation between IQ results and grades? Correlation can be positive or negative in results.

Research Vocabulary

Clinical Psychologist: Usually has a doctoral degree in psychology plus completes an internship. They cannot prescribe medicine.

Psychiatrist: A medical doctor with a degree who specializes in psychotherapy. Psychiatrists can prescribe drugs.

Ethics: Principals and standards of behavior, including morals. Determining what is right or wrong and having one's actions correlate with one's beliefs.

Endocrine System

The endocrine system is made up of the **hypothalamus** and other endocrine glands. Endocrine glands create and release chemicals into the bloodstream. The **pituitary gland** releases hormones that regulate the hormone secretions of other glands. The pituitary gland is located at the base of the skull and is about the size of a pea. Adrenal glands affect our moods, energy level and stress. Adrenal glands also secrete epinephrine (adrenaline) and norepinephrine.

The nervous system has an area called the **Autonomic Nervous System (ANS).** ANS works as an involuntary system; usually, we don't know it is there. Other involuntary systems include respiratory and cardiac functions. Here's the test: if you have to think about doing it, it's not involuntary. ANS is most important in the "fight or flight" response. When we experience large amounts of stress like in an emergency, our body gives us extra energy (adrenaline) to fight, perhaps against an attacker, or to take flight, to run from the attacker. In non-stress times, this system allows us to rest and digest.

This system is broken up into three different areas. These are:
- **sympathetic nervous system**: arousing part of the system
- **parasympathetic nervous system**: calming part of the system
- enteric nervous system

Limbic system: Structures in the cerebral cortex related to memory and emotion.

Hippocampus: Located in the limbic system. Its primary function is to store memories.

Cerebral cortex: The most developed part of the brain. Largest part of the brain (80%). Underneath the cerebral cortex are four lobes of the brain. These are:
- Occipital lobe: related to vision
- Temporal lobe: hearing
- Frontal lobe: voluntary muscles and intelligence
- Parietal lobe: body sensations

 Mental Health

There are a variety of mental health illnesses that need medication. The available medication has the ability to greatly improve the quality of life of the patient.

NDRI's, or norepinephrine and dopamine reuptake inhibitors, are a type of antidepressant medication. NDRI's increase the levels of norepinephrine and dopamine by stopping them from being reabsorbed into the cells. Norepinephrine and dopamine are neurons which relate stress and mood. By stopping them from reaching the cells, the person's mood is improved.

DSM-IV

The DSM-IV is the Diagnostic and Statistical Manual of Mental Disorders. It is published by the American Psychiatric Association. The DSM-IV has a list of mental disorders, their symptoms, causes, and statistics about them. It has been considered as the Bible of mental disorders by some. As time has progressed, there have been diseases added, and in some cases removed as more information becomes available. For example, homosexuality was removed from the DSM-IV.

 # Brain

The brain is a part of the central nervous system. It controls all necessary functions of the body. All emotions originate in the brain as well as memory and thought processes. It interprets signals from other parts of the body and turns those signals into rational thought such as, "My leg hurts from running too much." This developed brain is what makes us human by controlling our emotions, thoughts and consciousness.

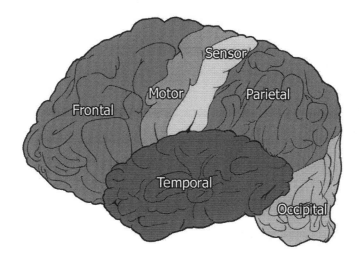

The brain is located in the skull. The skull protects this organ. There are also other things that protect the brain. There are three membranes that shield it. The outer layer, the dura mater, is the strongest and thickest. Beneath that layer is another membrane, called the arachnoid layer. Beneath that, the final layer, is the pia mater, which is mostly blood vessels. A clear fluid called cerebrospinal fluid covers the entire brain and is used to transport chemicals through the brain and to regulate pressure.

The brain and the spinal cord are the central nervous system. The cerebrum is the two large halves of the brain that you can see on the left. The deep "crack" in the middle is called the longitudinal fissure. The two halves of the brain communicate via bundles of axons called commissures. The largest commissure is called the corpus callosum.

Cerebrum: Houses memories and controls our responses to different sensory signals.

Cerebellum: Coordinates all movements and muscles.

Pons: Control breathing and heart rate.

Brain Stem: Sends commands to all other parts of the body.

Thalamus: Main relay station for incoming sensory signals to cerebral cortex and outgoing motor signals from it. All the senses but smell report to the thalamus.

Hypothalamus: Regulates internal temperature, eating, sleeping, drinking, emotions, and sexual activity.

Carbon Monoxide

Oxygen is carried through the body in blood cells by combining with oxygen carrying hemoglobin. When carbon monoxide enters the body, it combines with the hemoglobin to form carboxyhemoglobin (COHb). This means that the cells can no longer transport oxygen effectively, even to important organs such as the heart. This makes carbon monoxide an extremely dangerous chemical.

Sample Test Questions

1) Valium is on which drug Schedule?

   A) Schedule I
   B) Schedule II
   C) Schedule III
   D) Schedule IV

The correct answer is D:) Schedule IV.

2) Which of the following are risks of drug interaction?

   A) Cancellation of beneficial effects
   B) Possibility of lethal effects
   C) Cause unexpected side effects
   D) All of the above

The correct answer is D:) All of the above. Drug interactions have many possible outcomes which can render the used drugs useless to lethal.

3) Which of the following drugs most often has harmful interactions with other drugs being taken?

   A) Alcohol
   B) Aspirin
   C) Cocaine
   D) Nicotine

The correct answer is A:) Alcohol. Alcohol potentiates the effects of other drugs, commonly leading to serious and lethal effects.

4) Which act created drug scheduling?

   A) CAA
   B) CAS
   C) CSA
   D) CSS

The correct answer is C:) CSA. The Controlled Substances Act was passed in 1970.

5) What is cocaethylene?

    A) Alcohol + coatin
    B) Alcohol + cocaine
    C) Cocaine + ethyne
    D) Alcohol + ethyne

The correct answer is B:) Alcohol + cocaine. Cocaethylene is formed when cocaine and alcohol are taken simultaneously.

6) Which of the following does heroin function similarly to?

    A) Tylenol
    B) Methylphenidate
    C) Ibuprofen
    D) Morphine

The correct answer is D:) Morphine. The effects of morphine and heroin are identical. However, heroin is faster acting and more powerful. It is also an illegal substance in the United States.

7) What is the most common effect of drug interactions for psychoactive drugs?

    A) Decrease in respiratory rate
    B) Vomiting
    C) Irregular heartbeat
    D) Increase in blood pressure

The correct answer is A:) Decrease in respiratory rate. Most depressant drugs slow down the respiratory rate; taking these in combination causes additive effects which may result in death due to respiratory depression.

8) Which amendment to the U.S. constitution established prohibition?

    A) 20
    B) 21
    C) 18
    D) 16

The correct answer is C:) 18. The 18th amendment prohibited manufacture, sale, and transportation of alcohol within the United States.

9) Which of the following drugs should you give to someone suffering an acute asthma attack?

> A) Albuterol
> B) Zyflo oral
> C) Nasacort
> D) Brovana

The correct answer is A:) Albuterol. Albuterol is a bronchodilator which relaxes the air passageways and can be used to stop or prevent attacks.

10) At which cell location do drugs interact with the nervous system?

> A) At the axon
> B) At the dendrite
> C) At the neuron
> D) At the synapse

The correct answer is D:) At the synapse. The synaptic gap is the space between two neuron cells where interactions take place.

11) What is the general name for the chemical substance which triggers activity between neurons?

> A) Enzyme
> B) Vesicle
> C) Neurotransmitter
> D) Hormone

The correct answer is C:) Neurotransmitter. Neurotransmitters are the substance released by vesicles into the synaptic gap that interact with others neurons.

12) Which of the following is NOT a monoamine?

> A) Dopamine
> B) Serotinin
> C) Acetylcholine
> D) Norepinephrine

The correct answer is C:) Acetylcholine. Dopamine, serotonin, and norepinephrine are monoamines because their chemical structure consists of one amine group.

13) Which of the following is NOT true of cirrhosis?

    A) It is caused when the liver cells die and become scar tissue.
    B) Cirrhosis is easily reversible by discontinuing the use of alcohol.
    C) Once enough liver cells have died, Cirrhosis is not curable.
    D) As liver function decreases due to Cirrhosis, toxins build up in the body.

The correct answer is B:) Cirrhosis is easily reversible by discontinuing the use of alcohol. Both fatty liver and alcoholic hepatitis are reversible by abstaining from alcohol, but cirrhosis is not curable.

14) Which of the following is NOT a method that drugs interact with neurotransmitters?

    A) Neurotransmitter gathering
    B) Neurotransmitter synthesis
    C) Neurotransmitter degradation
    D) Neurotransmitter release

The correct answer is A:) Neurotransmitter gathering. Drugs can influence neurotransmitters to synthesize, transport, store, release, degrade, or reuptake.

15) What is uptake?

    A) A process where neurotransmitters are stored by neighboring cells
    B) A process which does not release neurotransmitters
    C) A process which gathers molecules from other cells
    D) A process where certain molecules are transmitted back to their release point

The correct answer is D:) A process where certain molecules are transmitted back to their release point. Uptake is the process where certain molecules are transmitted back to their release point.

16) Which of the following are effective techniques for crisis prevention pertaining to drug abuse?

    A) Consultation and arrest
    B) Ignorance and hospitalization
    C) Help-line and conversation
    D) Drug tests and denial

The correct answer is C:) Help-line and conversation. There are many techniques to prevent crises notably talking with the person and helping them understand the problem.

17) Which type of prevention focuses upon selected individuals who have been tested in some form to determine whether they should be included in a prevention group?

    A) Universal prevention
    B) Selective prevention
    C) Environmental prevention
    D) Indicated prevention

The correct answer is D:) Indicated prevention. Indicated prevention occurs when individuals have been screened by some criteria (social status, educational status, etc) in order to determine their relative risk of substance abuse.

18) What is the most commonly used illegal drug?

    A) Heroin
    B) LSD
    C) Marijuana
    D) PCP

The correct answer is C:) Marijuana.

19) Which drug is most responsible for causing Buerger's disease?

    A) Cocaine
    B) Tobacco
    C) Alcohol
    D) Methamphetamine

The correct answer is B:) Tobacco. Buerger's disease is commonly associated with smoking, but may also result from use of other tobacco products.

20) What is the highest percentage of alcohol a fermented beverage may contain without further processing?

    A) 15%
    B) 12%
    C) 20%
    D) 18%

The correct answer is A:) 15%. Fermented beverages cannot have more than 15% alcohol without further processing due to the fact that the yeasts that produce the ethanol reach a maximum at 15%.

21) What is the typical alcoholic percentage of table wine?

   A) 13%
   B) 15%
   C) 12%
   D) 8%

The correct answer is C:) 12%. Most table wines contain an alcoholic content of 12%.

22) Which of the following is NOT true of marijuana?

   A) Over 2000 chemicals are introduced to the body through smoking marijuana.
   B) Marijuana is a Schedule II drug because it has possible medical uses.
   C) Marijuana is illegal in the United States.
   D) Some people feel panicked and violent as a result of smoking marijuana, while others feel relaxed.

The correct answer is B:) Marijuana is a Schedule II drug because it has possible medical uses. Marijuana has no accepted medical uses and is considered a Schedule I drug.

23) Which of the following orders the alcoholic beverages correctly from highest alcoholic content to lowest?

   A) Rum, brandy, beer
   B) Vodka, wine, whisky
   C) Vodka, beer, wine
   D) Whiskey, rum, wine

The correct answer is A:) Rum, brandy, beer. Rum and vodka have the highest percentage contents followed by whiskey and brandy, then wine and beer.

24) Which of the following is not used to produce alcohol?

   A) Grapes
   B) Barley
   C) Potatoes
   D) Pork

The correct answer is D:) Pork. Grapes, barley, and potatoes are commonly used to make alcoholic beverages.

25) What enzyme is used in the liver to metabolize alcohol?

   A) Alcohol dehydrogenase
   B) Acetaldehyde
   C) Cytochrome enzymes
   D) The liver doesn't require any enzymes to metabolize alcohol.

The correct answer is A:) Alcohol dehydrogenase. It catalyzes the process of converting alcohol into a detoxified form.

26) What is the name of the function where a valve shuts down the transfer of alcohol from the stomach to the small intestine?

   A) Sphincter spasm
   B) Duodenum spasm
   C) Ethanospasm
   D) Pylorospasm

The correct answer is D:) Pylorospasm. Pylorospasm is the process where the pylorus closes off restricting alcohol to transfer to the small intestine. It usually occurs when very large amounts of alcohol are consumed.

27) What is proof?

   A) A third of the alcohol percentage
   B) Half of the alcohol percentage
   C) Double the alcohol percentage
   D) Triple the alcohol percentage

The correct answer is C:) Double the alcohol percentage. Proof is another way to measure the alcoholic content. It is double the alcoholic percentage of a beverage.

28) Approximately how many heroin users overdose per year?

   A) 3%
   B) 4%
   C) 5%
   D) 6%

The correct answer is A:) 3%.

29) What does BAC stand for?

    A) Blood alcohol contamination
    B) Blood average content
    C) Body alcohol content
    D) Blood alcohol content

The correct answer is D:) Blood alcohol content.

30) Which of the following is NOT true of anabolic steroids?

    A) Increased protein synthesis and bone density are effects of anabolic steroids.
    B) The effects of anabolic steroids include increased muscle mass and deepening voice.
    C) An athlete would most likely use anabolic steroids to increase their performance.
    D) They produce anabolic effects.

The correct answer is B:) The effects of anabolic steroids include increased muscle mass and deepening voice. While increased muscle mass is an effect of anabolic steroids, voice deepening is not.

31) What is the typical legal BAC content?

    A) .12%
    B) .10%
    C) .15%
    D) .13%

The correct answer is B:) .10%. The legal level of intoxication in most of the United States is .10%.

32) At what rate does the liver metabolize alcohol?

    A) .6 oz per hour
    B) 6 oz per hour
    C) .6 mL per hour
    D) 6 mL per hour

The correct answer is A:) .6 oz per hour. This is the amount of alcohol in about one drink.

33) Which of the following is NOT a common way to measure BAC?

    A) Blood sample
    B) Breath sample
    C) Perspiration sample
    D) Urine sample

The correct answer is C:) Perspiration sample. BAC is most commonly established through a breath test, although blood and urine samples are also used.

34) Which of the following can help someone become sober faster?

    A) Eating
    B) Drinking coffee
    C) Exercising
    D) None of the above

The correct answer is D:) None of the above. The body metabolizes alcohol at a constant rate that cannot be modified.

35) Which of the following is NOT an effect of anabolic steroids?

    A) Increased muscle mass
    B) Increased protein synthesis
    C) Increased bone density
    D) Deepened voice

The correct answer is D:) Deepened voice. Voice deepening is an example of an androgenic effect.

36) Which other types of drugs does alcohol share a cross-tolerance with?

    A) Barbiturates
    B) Amphetamines
    C) Phencyclidine
    D) Mescaline

The correct answer is A:) Barbiturates. Alcohol shares a cross-tolerance with barbiturates and other depressant drugs.

37) Which two organs are most affected by long-term heavy drinking?

    A) Kidneys and liver
    B) Stomach and liver
    C) Brain and liver
    D) Brain and kidneys

The correct answer is C:) Brain and liver. Long-term alcohol use affects all of the body's organ, but most specifically the brain and liver where permanent damage can become fatal.

38) Which of the following syndromes is NOT a result of alcohol usage?

    A) Fetal alcohol syndrome
    B) Asperger syndrome
    C) Wernicke syndrome
    D) Korsakoff syndrome

The correct answer is B:) Asperger syndrome. Fetal alcohol syndrome, Wernicke syndrome, and Korsakoff syndrome all have heavy alcoholic usage as a main factor.

39) Which of the following is NOT an Alcoholic Liver Disease (ALD)?

    A) Sickle cell disease
    B) Fatty liver
    C) Alcoholic hepatitis
    D) Cirrhosis

The correct answer is A:) Sickle cell disease. Sickle cell disease is a genetic condition in which a person's blood cells become rigid and deformed. Fatty liver, alcoholic hepatitis and cirrhosis are all liver diseases.

40) What is the term for a temporary state in which a person is physically and psychologically impaired because of a toxin affecting the central nervous system?

    A) Blackout
    B) Intoxication
    C) Seizure
    D) Disabled

The correct answer is B:) Intoxication. Intoxication is a temporary state in which a person is physically and psychologically impaired because of a toxin affecting the central nervous system.

41) Which of the following is NOT an effect caused by alcohol?

    A) Short-term memory loss
    B) Disruption of sleep patterns
    C) More frequent urges to urinate
    D) Decrease in appetite

The correct answer is D:) Decrease in appetite. Alcohol increases gastric secretion which in turn increases appetite.

42) Which of the following is NOT a symptom of Korsakoff's syndrome?

    A) Anterograde amnesia
    B) Retrograde amnesia
    C) Short term memory loss
    D) Confabulation

The correct answer is C:) Short term memory loss. People with Korsakoff's syndrome generally retain their short term memory, although they lose other types of memory.

43) Which of the following is the worst way to treat a hangover?

    A) Exercising
    B) Taking an analgesic
    C) Drinking alcohol
    D) Taking tranquilizers

The correct answer is C:) Drinking alcohol. Drinking alcohol to cure a hangover is the worst way to treat this condition because it can establish a habit of heavy drinking. It also is unadvised because it does not "cure" the hangover, just delays it.

44) Which of the following is NOT true of Narcan?

    A) Narcan is also called naloxone hydrochloride.
    B) It works by blocking the opiate receptors in the body.
    C) Narcan is used exclusively in emergency situations.
    D) Narcan is used to counter addiction problems as well as in emergency situations.

The correct answer is C:) Narcan is used exclusively in emergency situations. While Narcan is used in emergency situations, it is also used in long term situations.

45) Which of the following does not potentiate the effects of alcohol?

    A) Fluvoxamines
    B) Barbiturates
    C) Benzodiazepines
    D) Antihistamines

The correct answer is A:) Fluvoxamines. Barbiturates, benzodiazepines, and antihistamines all combine and increase the effects of alcohol. Special attention is needed because combing barbiturates and benzodiazepines with alcohol can result in death.

46) At what BAC level are gross motor functions (standing, walking) obviously impaired?

    A) 8%
    B) 15%
    C) 5%
    D) 10%

The correct answer is B:) 15%. At 15% BAC a person has trouble standing without swaying and walking in a straight line.

47) What are the labels for axes in a dose-response curve?

    A) X-axis: dose y-axis: number of drugs
    B) X-axis: dose y-axis: response
    C) X-axis: response y-axis: dose
    D) X-axis: response y-axis: number of drugs

The correct answer is B:) X-axis: dose y-axis: response. In a dose-response curve the x-axis represents the drug dosage and the y-axis represents the response to the given dosage.

48) What of the following cannot be determined from a dose-response curve?

    A) Drug potency
    B) Maximal effect
    C) Effective dose
    D) Side effects

The correct answer is D:) Side effects. Side effects cannot be determined from a dose-response curve, although the potency of side effects can be charted.

49) What Schedule is heroin included in?

    A) Schedule I
    B) Schedule II
    C) Schedule III
    D) Schedule IV

The correct answer is A:) Schedule I. Heroin is highly addictive, unsafe and has no accepted medical purpose.

50) What is the process in which the body breaks down drugs into simpler components and waste products?

    A) Metabolism
    B) Absorption
    C) Distribution
    D) Reuptake

The correct answer is A:) Metabolism. Metabolism is the process in which the body breaks down drugs in order to detoxify itself.

51) What is another name for Xanax?

    A) Alprazolam
    B) Diazepam
    C) Valium
    D) Narcan

The correct answer is A:) Alprazolam.

52) Which of the following organs is the one that predominantly metabolizes drugs?

    A) Liver
    B) Kidney
    C) Lungs
    D) Stomach

The correct answer is A:) Liver. The liver is the organ which predominantly detoxifies the body of drugs and other matter. It has high concentrations of enzymes which break down drugs and is one of the first organs to react to drugs that have entered into the digestive organs.

53) Which of the following correctly lists the rate of delivery of drugs into the body from faster to slowest for psychoactive drugs?

    A) Injection, oral ingestion, inhalation
    B) Inhalation, injection, oral ingestion
    C) Inhalation, oral ingestion, injection
    D) Injection, inhalation, oral ingestion

The correct answer is B:) Inhalation, injection, oral ingestion. For psychoactive drugs, inhalation is the fastest way to get the drug in the body followed by injection and then oral ingestion.

54) Which two federal agencies determine what schedule a drug is classified as?

    A) DEA and FDA
    B) FAA and FDA
    C) DEA and FAA
    D) DAE and FDA

The correct answer is A:) DEA and FDA. The Drug Enforcement Administration and Food and Drug Administration are the type agencies which determine scheduling.

55) Which of the following drugs will have the longest lasting effects?

    A) A small dose of a low protein binding drug
    B) A small dose of a high protein binding drug
    C) A large dose of a low protein binding drug
    D) A large dose of a high protein binding drug

The correct answer is D:) A large dose of a high protein binding drug. A high binding drug will last longer than a low binding drug because fewer molecules will be available for metabolization. A large dose will last longer than a smaller one because it will take longer for the large dose to be metabolized.

56) Which of the following is NOT generally a side effect of benzodiazepines?

    A) Drowsiness
    B) Hallucinations
    C) Nausea
    D) Blurry vision

The correct answer is B:) Hallucinations. Benzodiazepines are relaxants, and drowsiness, nausea, and blurry vision are all common side effects attributed to them.

57) The 1938 Food, Drug, and Cosmetic Act enforced which of the following?

    A) Drug labels to frankly list ingredients
    B) Drug distributors to federally register
    C) Drug manufacturers to submit a NDA
    D) Drug testing to be pre-approved

The correct answer is C:) Drug manufactures to submit a NDA. The 1938 Food, Drug, and Cosmetic Act required that manufacturers submit a NDA (new drug application) so that the product could be approved by the FDA (Food and Drug Administration) before being publicly marketed.

58) What Schedule is marijuana included in?

    A) Schedule V
    B) Schedule IV
    C) Schedule II
    D) Schedule I

The correct answer is D:) Schedule I.

59) Which act first distinguished between prescription and over-the-counter drugs?

    A) The 1914 Harrison Act
    B) The 1938 Food, Drug, and Cosmetic Act
    C) The 1962 Kefauver-Harris amendments
    D) The 1906 Pure Food and Drugs Act

The correct answer is B:) The 1938 Food, Drug, and Cosmetic Act. The 1938 Food, Drug, and Cosmetic Act was the first act to distinguish whether or not a drug was to only be used after a physician's recommendation.

60) Before a drug may be released to the market on who must it be previously tested?

    A) Three animal species and non-healthy humans
    B) Two animal species, healthy humans, and non-healthy humans
    C) Healthy humans and non-healthy humans
    D) One animal species, healthy humans, and non-healthy humans

The correct answer is B:) Two animal species, healthy humans, and non-healthy humans. Before a drug can be approved for the market it must be first tested thoroughly on two different species of animals, healthy humans, and humans with the condition that it is hoping to treat.

61) Which of the following did NOT result from the Comprehensive Drug Abuse Prevention and Control Act of 1970?

   A) Creation of the Director of National Drug Control Policy
   B) Update of all prior laws dealing with drugs
   C) Establishment of five schedules of drugs
   D) Increase in penalties for possession

The correct answer is A:) Creation of the Director of National Drug Control Policy. The Director of National Drug Control Policy was not instituted until the 1988 Omnibus Drug Act.

62) Which government organization currently is occupied with enforcing drug related laws?

   A) The FDA
   B) The DEA
   C) The FBI
   D) The DFA

The correct answer is B:) The DEA. The DEA (Drug Enforcement Administration) is the organization that is concerned with drug related issues.

63) How is alcohol metabolized?

   A) Alcohol isn't metabolized, the liver just absorbs the alcohol.
   B) The liver converts the alcohol using an enzyme called alcohol dehydrogenase.
   C) It kidney converts the alcohol using cytochrome enzymes.
   D) The liver converts the alcohol using cytochrome enzymes.

The correct answer is B:) The liver converts the alcohol using an enzyme called alcohol dehydrogenase.

64) Which of the following best defines psychoactive drugs?

   A) Drugs which cause a person to hallucinate.
   B) Drugs which directly affect the brain.
   C) Drug which speed up or slow down the nervous system.
   D) Any drug which does not directly affect the brain.

The correct answer is B:) Drugs which directly affect the brain. Although A and C correctly identify types of psychoactive drugs, Answer B is the best definition of psychoactive drugs as a whole.

65) The mesolimbic pathway is a main passageway for which of the following neurotransmitters?

A) Dopamine
B) Keratime
C) Serotonin
D) Acetylcholine

The correct answer is A:) Dopamine. The mesolimbic pathway is an important dopamine pathway that starts at the midbrain and continues into the forebrain. This pathway is said to be mainly responsible for drug addiction.

66) Which of the following neurotransmitters is NOT associated with drug use?

A) Samatostatin
B) Acetylcholine
C) Nor-epinephrine
D) Serotonin

The correct answer is A:) Samatostatin. Samatostatin is a neurotransmitter that inhibits the release of other hormones. It is not associated with drug usage.

67) The ANS (autonomic nervous system) contains which of the following branches?

A) Systematic and nonsystematic
B) Sensitive and non-sensitive
C) Sensory and parasensory
D) Sympathetic and parasympathetic

The correct answer is D:) Sympathetic and parasympathetic. The ANS is divided into two branches, the sympathetic and the parasympathetic.

68) Which of the following is NOT a characteristic of Schedule I drugs?

A) Highly addictive
B) Accepted medical use
C) Unsafe
D) No accepted medical use

The correct answer is B:) Accepted medical use. Although this describes each of the other four schedules, Schedule V drugs have no accepted medical use.

69) Which of the following is associated with the "flight of fight" reaction?

    A) The somatic system
    B) The sympathetic system
    C) The parasympathetic system
    D) The enteric system

The correct answer is B:) The sympathetic system. The sympathetic system is the system within the ANS (autonomic nervous system) that reacts in a "flight of fight" manner, such as a dilation of the pupils, an increase in the heart rate, etc.

70) How is alcohol eliminated from the body?

    A) Alcohol is absorbed by the liver. When enough builds up, the liver just stops working.
    B) When the alcohol has been in the blood stream for a while it just dissolves.
    C) Alcohol must be metabolized by the liver.
    D) Alcohol cannot be eliminated from the body, just absorbed by the kidneys.

The correct answer is C:) Alcohol must be metabolized by the liver. This happens at a rate of .6 oz per hour.

71) A lack of acetylcholine in the cerebral cortex has been linked with which of the following diseases?

    A) Parkinson's disease
    B) Addison's disease
    C) Huntington's disease
    D) Alzheimer's disease

The correct answer is D:) Alzheimer's disease. Alzheimer's disease has been linked with a lack of acetylcholine in the cerebral cortex.

72) Drug doses are determined principally by which factor?

    A) Age
    B) Weight
    C) Height
    D) Degree of need

The correct answer is B:) Weight. Drug doses are determined by weight and the normal unit is drug per kilogram.

73) How is a drug's therapeutic index related to its safety?

    A) The higher the therapeutic index is, the safer the drug is.
    B) The lower the therapeutic index is, the safer the drug is.
    C) The higher the therapeutic index is, the more dangerous the drug is.
    D) There is no relation between therapeutic index and safety.

The correct answer is A:) The higher the therapeutic index is, the safer the drug is. This is because a higher therapeutic index indicates a greater amount between the lethal dose and effective dose.

74) Which of the following is NOT a group of barbiturates?

    A) Slow acting
    B) Intermediate acting
    C) Medium acting
    D) Long acting

The correct answer is C:) Medium acting. The three groups of barbiturates are slow acting, intermediate acting, and long acting.

75) Which of the following is NOT influenced by the route by which drugs are taken?

    A) Drug distribution speed
    B) Type of high reached
    C) How long drug effects last
    D) Degree of addiction

The correct answer is D:) Degree of addiction. The method that one chooses to take drugs influences how quickly the drug is distributed in the body, the high that is reached, and the length of the drug experience.

76) Which of the following is NOT a basic category of psychoactive drugs?

    A) Depressant
    B) Hallucinogen
    C) Elevator
    D) Stimulant

The correct answer is C:) Elevator. Depressants, hallucinogens and stimulants are the three types of psychoactive drugs.

77) Which of the following methods of drug administration is considered the safest?

A) Inhalation
B) Injection
C) Membrane absorption
D) Oral

The correct answer is D:) Oral. Taking drugs orally is one of the safest routes as it is convenient and has the slowest absorption rate.

78) What is the term for the transportation of a drug to a certain site?

A) Feedback
B) Distribution
C) Absorption
D) Transportation

The correct answer is B:) Distribution. Distribution is the term used to describe the action of a drug being transported to different sites in the body.

79) What does DSM-IV stand for?

A) Doctor's Safety Manual for IV's
B) Driver Safety Manual Fourth Edition
C) Diagnostic and Statistical Manual of Mental Disorders
D) Diagnostic and Statistical Model Fourth Edition

The correct answer is C:) Diagnostic and Statistical Manual of Mental Disorders.

80) What is the formula for Blood Alcohol Content (BAC)?

A) BAC=NHD×.03 - NSD×.02.
B) BAC=NSD×.02 - NHD×.02.
C) BAC=NSD×.02 - NHD×.03.
D) BAC=NSD×.03 - NHD×.02.

The correct answer is D:) BAC=NSD×.03 - NHD×.02.

81) Which of the following is NOT an effect of a drug leaving the body?

    A) End of drug experience
    B) Rebound of earlier effects
    C) Desire to take more drugs
    D) Detoxification of blood

The correct answer is A:) End of drug experience. When a drug leave the body it often is not the end of the drug experience and triggers other effects.

82) Which of the following biological factors does NOT effect the reaction of an individual to a drug?

    A) Gender
    B) Genetics
    C) Age
    D) Height

The correct answer is D:) Height. Height does not affect a person's reaction to a drug, while gender, genetics, and age all influence the drug experience.

83) What drug caused many birth defects before it was removed from the market?

    A) Valium
    B) Diazepam
    C) Thalidomide
    D) Acetaldehyde

The correct answer is C:) Thalidomide. Though widely distributed during the 1950's as a medication for morning sickness, Thalidomide was removed from the market in the late 1960's.

84) What is homeostasis?

    A) A system which is stable because all components are the same
    B) A state of balance which tries to restore itself if disrupted
    C) A state in which the body does not function because of same-same reaction
    D) A system where the body is constantly changing

The correct answer is B:) A state of balance which tries to restore itself if disrupted.

85) What is the maximum BAC at which a person is allowed to drive in the United States?

    A) 8% BAC
    B) .8% BAC
    C) .08% BAC
    D) .008% BAC

The correct answer is C:) .08% BAC. If a person's BAC is any higher than that, they are not legally allowed to drive.

86) Which of the following statements is TRUE?

    A) Tolerance can be reversed
    B) Tolerance to a drug is developed at a constant rate
    C) All drugs are subject to tolerance
    D) Tolerance is caused because of psychological reasons

The correct answer is A:) Tolerance can be reversed. Tolerance is developed at different rates according to the drug type and individual factors; however it can be reversed.

87) What is synesthesia?

    A) When a person's perception of two or more senses becomes mixed.
    B) When a person consumes something that is plastic.
    C) Another name for protein synthesis.
    D) When a person is unable to determine reality from fantasy.

The correct answer is A:) When a person's perception of two or more senses becomes mixed. Synesthesia is a common effect of hallucinogenic drugs.

88) Which of the following groups are used to verify the result of certain drug tests are not just psychological?

    A) Control group
    B) Placebo group
    C) Animal group
    D) Psychological group

The correct answer is B:) Placebo group. Placebo groups are used in drug testing to verify that results are not a result of belief that one is taking a drug that will have certain effects. Often the experiment is done double-bind, so that neither the experimenter nor the test subjects know who is in the placebo group.

89) Which of the following is a Schedule II drug?

    A) Heroin
    B) Cocaine
    C) Marijuana
    D) All of the above

The correct answer is B:) Cocaine. Cocaine is a Schedule II drug, while Heroin and Marijuana are considered Schedule I drugs.

90) Which of the follow is a problem which was caused by Thalidomide?

    A) Mental disorders
    B) Deformed limbs
    C) Addiction
    D) Fetal alcohol syndrome

The correct answer is B:) Deformed limbs.

91) How many chemicals are released when a cigarette is burned?

    A) At least 46
    B) Less than 400
    C) About 500
    D) Over 4,000

The correct answer is D:) Over 4,000. At least 46 of these chemicals are carcinogens.

92) Which category of drug is currently used as the primary choice for a sedative hypnotic?

    A) Benzodiazepines
    B) Amphetamines
    C) Barbiturates
    D) Hallucinogens

The correct answer is A:) Benzodiazepines. In the past barbiturates were used as sedative hypnotic drugs, but have been replaced by benzodiazepines which are considered safer.

93) Who produces the DSM-IV?

   A) World Health Organization
   B) American Doctor's Association
   C) American Psychiatric Association
   D) Agency for the Safety of Mammals

The correct answer is C:) American Psychiatric Association.

94) Why has prescribed use of barbiturates declined?

   A) Ineffectiveness of drug
   B) Dangerous side effects
   C) Rapid tolerance development
   D) Prescribed use has not declined

The correct answer is C:) Rapid tolerance development. Barbiturates are no longer used as sedative hypnotics because of rapid tolerance development. A user goes through a withdrawal similar to that of alcohol which cancels the benefits the drug may have had.

95) Which of the following is NOT a stage of detoxification?

   A) Introduction of toxin
   B) Cleaning the body of toxins
   C) Removal of dead cells
   D) Rebuilding of damaged tissues

The correct answer is A:) Introduction of toxin. Detoxification is the removal of harmful toxins, not the introduction.

96) Which of the following is NOT true about heroin overdose?

   A) Combining heroin with other types of substance abuse heightens the risk of overdose.
   B) Approximately 3% of heroin users overdose per year.
   C) Heroin users have an increased risk of developing respiratory and hepatic disease.
   D) It is not possible for a person's heroin tolerance to decrease.

The correct answer is D:) It is not possible for a person's heroin tolerance to decrease. When a person abstains from heroin for a period of time their tolerance decreases. This is one reason why people overdose.

97) What is NOT a common problem of using sedative hypnotics?

    A) Rapid addiction
    B) Risk of overdose
    C) Severe withdrawal symptoms
    D) Anxiety

The correct answer is D:) Anxiety. A person using sedative hypnotics will not have anxiety symptoms as they are depressants and help relieve anxiety.

98) What does elevated hepatic enzymes levels indicate?

    A) Higher than average liver health
    B) Higher than average liver function
    C) Liver damage
    D) Nothing is indicated by elevated hepatic enzyme levels

The correct answer is C:) Liver damage. Higher than average levels of hepatic enzymes indicate liver damage, often as a result of substance abuse.

99) How do NDRI's work?

    A) NDRI's stop certain neurons from being able to communicate with the brain.
    B) NDRI's both quicken some neurons, and slow other from reach the brain.
    C) NDRI's help some types of neurons reach the cells more easily.
    D) NDRI's stop certain neurons from being able to reach a person's cells.

The correct answer is D:) NDRI's stop certain neurons from being able to reach a person's cells. By stopping norepinephrine and dopamine from reach the cells, NDRI's work as a type of antidepressant.

100) What are carcinogens?

    A) The term for any chemical that is in a cigarette.
    B) Chemicals in the body which protect it from cancer causing bacteria.
    C) Chemicals which are known to cause cancer.
    D) The term for the many non-cancer causing chemicals in cigarettes.

The correct answer is C:) Chemicals which are known to cause cancer.

101) Which of the following drugs does NOT share cross tolerance with the others?

A) Benzodiazepines
B) Alcohol
C) LSD
D) Methaqualone

The correct answer is C:) LSD. Benzodiazepines, alcohol, and methaqualone are all cross-tolerant as well as other sedatives and barbiturates.

102) Which of the following is NOT true of carbon monoxide?

A) When carbon monoxide enters the body it combines to form carboxyhemoglobin.
B) Carbon monoxide makes the blood cells less able to transport oxygen through the body.
C) Carbon monoxide combines with oxygen carrying hemoglobin.
D) It is not dangerous to be exposed to carbon monoxide for long periods of time.

The correct answer is D:) It is not dangerous to be exposed to carbon monoxide for long period of time. Carbon monoxide can be extremely dangerous with extended exposure because it reduces the circulation of oxygen through the body.

103) For which of the following was peyote NOT used in Native American culture?

A) To heal the sick and injured.
B) To cause the user to have visions.
C) To commune with the spirit world.
D) Peyote was not used at all in the Native American culture.

The correct answer is D:) Peyote was not used at all in the Native American culture. Peyote was used in the Native American culture for social, cultural, and religious purposes.

104) Which of the following is a non-beneficial effect of benzodiazepines?

A) Rapid addiction
B) Anterograde amnesia
C) Low lethal doses
D) Long duration

The correct answer is B:) Anterograde amnesia. Benzodiazepines do not cause rapid addiction, are not very lethal, and there effects have a long duration; however after having taken benzodiazepines, patients may experience bouts of amnesia following drug treatment.

105) Cocaine is used medicinally in which situation?

    A) Increased circulation and blood flow
    B) Numbing of the lowe extremities
    C) Numbing of the upper respiratory tract
    D) No known medicinal use

The correct answer is C:) Numbing of the upper respiratory tract. Cocaine or Cocaine hydrochloride solution is also used to reduce bleeding of the mucous membranes in the mouth, throat, and nasal cavities. However, better products have been developed for these purposes, and cocaine is rarely used medically in the United States.

106) Which of the following contains sedative and pain relieving components which depress the central nervous system?

    A) Narcotics
    B) Depressants
    C) Hallucinogens
    D) Stimulants

The correct answer is A:) Narcotics. A narcotic is a CNS depressant that contains sedatives and pain relieving components.

107) Which of the following is NOT a narcotic?

    A) Heroin
    B) Mescaline
    C) Opium
    D) Codeine

The correct answer is B:) Mescaline. Mescaline is a hallucinogen; the others are all forms of narcotics.

108) Which of the following is TRUE of benzodiazepines?

    A) Benzodiazepines work by decreasing brain function, and as the dose increases so do the side effects.
    B) Benzodiazepines are considered the least abused pharmaceutical drug.
    C) Benzodiazepines almost always cause sever complications due to overdose.
    D) Benzodiazepines are used to counter depression and tiredness.

The correct answer is A:) Benzodiazepines work by decreasing brain function, and as the dose increases so do the side effects. Answers B, C, and D all state essentially the opposite of what is true.

109) When two acetyl groups are attached to morphine which of the following drugs result?

    A) Codeine
    B) Methadone
    C) Heroin
    D) Mescaline

The correct answer is C:) Heroin. Heroin results from an addition of two acetyl groups to morphine. It is the same drug, but more potent.

110) What is naloxone?

    A) A narcotic with effects similar to codeine
    B) A highly toxic narcotic
    C) A hallucinogen
    D) A narcotic blocker

The correct answer is D:) A narcotic blocker. Naloxone is a narcotic antagonist which blocks narcotic drug actions.

111) What is Korsakoff's syndrome caused by?

    A) Vitamin c deficiency
    B) An excess of thiamine
    C) Old age
    D) Thiamine deficiency

The correct answer is D:) Thiamine deficiency. Korsakoff's syndrome is caused by a deficiency of thiamine, or vitamin B, in the brain.

112) Which of the following is the most life-threatening effect of narcotic use?

    A) Brain damage
    B) Drowsiness
    C) Respiratory depression
    D) Nausea

The correct answer is C:) Respiratory depression. With high overdoses of narcotics, users often enter into deep respiratory depression and simply stop breathing and die.

113) Which type of drugs cause formication syndrome?

    A) Narcotics
    B) Depressants
    C) Hallucinogens
    D) Stimulants

The correct answer is D:) Stimulants. Stimulants such as cocaine and amphetamine used in high amounts cause formication syndrome, an itchy feeling of insects crawling over the skin.

114) Which of the following is a withdrawal symptom of LSD?

    A) Vomiting
    B) Depression
    C) Muscle cramps
    D) There are no known withdrawal symptoms of LSD

The correct answer is D:) There are no known withdrawal symptoms of LSD. LSD does not seem to have withdrawal symptoms.

115) Which of the following is NOT a withdrawal symptom of PCP?

    A) Nausea
    B) Violence
    C) Muscle rigidity
    D) Coma

The correct answer is A:) Nausea. Violence, muscle rigidity, coma, and convulsions are all withdrawal symptoms of PCP.

116) What is another name for Valium?

    A) Diazepam
    B) Narcan
    C) Xanax
    D) Chlordiazepoxide

The correct answer is A:) Diazepam. Valium is commonly used as a relaxant.

117) Which of the following correctly lists the drug high duration of cocaine by various administration methods from longest to shortest?

    A) Nasal inhalation, injection, chewed, smoked
    B) Chewed, nasal inhalation, injection, smoked
    C) Chewed, nasal inhalation, smoked, injection
    D) Nasal inhalation, chewed, injection, smoked

The correct answer is B:) Chewed, nasal inhalation, injection, smoked. When chewed the high is not as strong, but lasts the longest while smoking produces the fastest high but fades the fastest.

118) Which of the following are all effects of stimulant use?

    A) Sleeplessness, weight loss, alertness
    B) Arousal, sleeplessness, intellectual enhancement
    C) Depression, weight loss, analgesic
    D) Alertness, arousal, depression

The correct answer is A:) Sleeplessness, weight loss, alertness. Stimulants decrease the desire to sleep, help weight loss, and cause heightened alertness.

119) Which of the following effects do NOT result from high cocaine dosage?

    A) Psychotic state
    B) Death
    C) Seizures
    D) Exhaustion

The correct answer is D:) Exhaustion. High cocaine dosage can result in a psychotic state, death, and seizures.

120) Which of the following is another name for naloxone hydrochloride?

    A) NHC
    B) NalHyd
    C) Naloxide
    D) Narcan

The correct answer is D:) Narcan.

121) Which of the following is Valium NOT used for?

    A) Alcohol withdrawal
    B) Seizures
    C) Anxiety
    D) Heart failure

The correct answer is D:) Heart failure. Valium is used as a relaxant. Alcohol withdrawal, seizures, and anxiety are all cases in which Valium might be used.

122) Which of the following is NOT a direct effect of caffeine?

    A) Stimulation of gastric acid
    B) Muscle fatigue
    C) Diuresis
    D) Stimulation of the heart

The correct answer is B:) Muscle fatigue. Caffeine effects the stimulation of gastric acid, diuresis, and stimulation of the heart.

123) Which of the following is NOT a property of Xanax?

    A) Sedative
    B) Hypnotic
    C) Slow onset
    D) Muscle relaxant

The correct answer is C:) Slow onset. Xanax has a relatively fast onset and has sedative, hypnotic and muscle relaxant properties.

124) Who discovered LSD (d-Lysergic Acid Diethylamide)?

    A) The Austrian
    B) The German
    C) The Swiss Hofmann
    D) The American Hulman

The correct answer is C:) The Swiss Hofmann. Hofmann discovered LSD in 1943 when he was synthesizing chemicals derived from ergot alkaloids.

125) What is an effective dose of LSD?

    A) 250 mg
    B) 50 mg
    C) 150 mg
    D) 100 mg

The correct answer is B:) 50 mg. An effective dose of LSD is very small 50 mg is all that is needed.

126) How is therapeutic index calculated?

    A) LD50/LE50
    B) LE50/ED50
    C) ED50/LD50
    D) LD50/ED50

The correct answer is D:) LD50/ED50. This is also known as the "lethal dose" divided by the "effective dose."

127) What is the term for the incidence where senses blend (seeing sound)?

    A) Sensethesia
    B) Sensacontraria
    C) Synesation
    D) Synesthesia

The correct answer is D:) Synesthesia. Synesthesia is the term for when senses blend. This is often experienced when using hallucinogens.

128) Which of the following hallucinogens does NOT occur naturally?

    A) Psilocybin
    B) DMT
    C) LSD
    D) Mescaline

The correct answer is C:) LSD. LSD does not occur in nature. It can only be synthesized chemically.

129) Which hallucinogen most frequently alters an individual's perception of their body?

    A) PCP
    B) Mescaline
    C) LSD
    D) MDA

The correct answer is A:) PCP. A person taking PCP will often be disoriented concerning their body and unsure what part is what or may feel completely disconnected with their body.

130) What is pharmacotherapy?

    A) Counseling given by a pharmacist
    B) Using drugs to help treat addiction
    C) Treatment of addiction by complete withdrawal
    D) Monitored drug usage

The correct answer is B:) Using drugs to help treat addiction. Pharmacotherapy is a treatment to help overcome drug addiction by using drugs.

131) Which of the following is TRUE of cannabis?

    A) C. sativa and C. indica are the only types of cannabis with psychoactive properties.
    B) C. indica is the only type of cannabis with psychoactive properties.
    C) C. diazepalis is the only type of cannabis which does not have psychoactive properties.
    D) All types of cannabis have psychoactive properties.

The correct answer is D:) All types of cannabis have psychoactive properties. C. sativa, C. indica, and C ruderalis all have psychoactive properties. C. diazepalis is not a real plant.

132) Which of the following is NOT a type of cannabis?

    A) Cannabis sativa
    B) Cannabis ruderalis
    C) Cannabis diazepalis
    D) Cannabis indica

The correct answer is C:) Cannabis diazepalis. The three types of cannabis plants are C. sativa, C. indica, and C. ruderalis.

133) Which of the following is NOT true?

    A) Alcohol is considered safe to drink during the first two months of pregnancy.
    B) There is no known safe time to drink while pregnant.
    C) It is not recommended that a woman drink while pregnant.
    D) There is no known safe amount of alcohol to drink while pregnant.

The correct answer is A:) Alcohol is considered safe to drink during the first two months of pregnancy. It is not considered safe to drink at any time during pregnancy, and for this reason it is recommended that women who are sexually active and not on birth control do not drink.

134) What is detoxification?

    A) There is no such thing as detoxification.
    B) When the body rebuilds tissue damage caused by toxins.
    C) When the body repairs damage caused by toxins.
    D) The process by which the body rids itself of harmful toxins.

The correct answer is D:) The process by which the body rids itself of harmful toxins. Answers B and C both give steps of detoxification, but Answer D defines it.

135) Which of the following factors most influences whether drug addiction treatment will be successful?

    A) Professional treatment
    B) Length of addiction
    C) Number of treatment techniques used
    D) Personality and environment

The correct answer is D:) Personality and environment. The personality and environment seem to have the greatest effect on whether an addict will successfully remain away from drug use.

136) What must occur in order for a drug to affect the brain?

    A) Be administered by injection
    B) Affect no other organs
    C) Infect a chemical pathway
    D) Pass the blood-brain barrier

The correct answer is D:) Pass the blood-brain barrier. A drug cannot affect the brain unless it can pass through the blood-brain barrier, a protection system of the brain.

137) In what organ are hepatic enzymes found?

A) Liver
B) Kidney
C) Heart
D) Lungs

The correct answer is A:) Liver. Hepatic enzymes are enzymes in the liver which indicate liver damage.

138) When in the brain, drugs:

A) Defuse into neurotransmitters only
B) Defuse everywhere
C) Defuse according to their type into certain pathways
D) Do not leave the bloodstream

The correct answer is B:) Defuse everywhere. When in the brain drugs don't know where to go exactly and defuse into the whole brain. However, they affect only the receptors that assimilate their chemical structure.

139) What is the term for a concentration of drug at a specific location of available reactivity within the body?

A) Bioavailability
B) Dose concentration
C) Percent reactive
D) Drug index

The correct answer is A:) Bioavailability. Bioavailability is the term for a concentration of drug at a specific location of available reactivity within the body.

140) Which of the following is TRUE of barbiturates?

A) Slow acting barbiturates take effect very quickly.
B) Barbiturates have largely replaced more dangerous benzodiazepines.
C) All types of barbiturates take effect within about 20 minutes.
D) Some barbiturates depress a person's system, while some stimulate it.

The correct answer is A:) Slow acting barbiturates take effect very quickly. There are also intermediate acting and long acting barbiturates.

141) When taken with food in the stomach, a drug:

   A) Will have no effect
   B) Will have a greater effect
   C) Will be absorbed slower
   D) Will be absorbed faster

The correct answer is C:) Will be absorbed slower.

142) What does NDRI stand for?

   A) Norepinephrine and dopamine reuptake inhibitors
   B) Neuron and dopamine reuptake inhibitors
   C) Norepinephrine and depression reuptake inhibitors
   D) Neuron and depression reuptake inhibitors

The correct answer is A:) Norepinephrine and dopamine reuptake inhibitors. NDRI's are a type of antidepressant medication.

143) Why does a drug passing through the lungs have rapid effects?

   A) Very accessible capillary walls
   B) Remains in blood for long period of time
   C) Bypasses the heart
   D) Deposits large quantities in the blood

The correct answer is A:) Very accessible capillary walls. A drug entering through the lungs quickly rejoins the bloodstream and passes quickly through the heart to the brain.

144) Which organ in human anatomy is the most complex?

   A) Lungs
   B) Intestines
   C) Heart
   D) Brain

The correct answer is D:) Brain. The brain is the most complex human organ that is one of the most amazing existing functional systems.

145) Which organ removes drugs from the body?

    A) Stomach
    B) Kidney
    C) Brain
    D) Lungs

The correct answer is B:) Kidney. The kidney and liver remove drugs from the bloodstream and process them so they leave the body.

146) Which organ most affects the distribution of drug in the body?

    A) Stomach
    B) Lung
    C) Heart
    D) Brain

The correct answer is C:) Heart. The heart is responsible for the transport of blood throughout the body. Drugs move throughout the body by means of the bloodstream, so the heart moves them around.

147) What is the fastest way to take a drug?

    A) Through an IV
    B) Orally
    C) Through the nose
    D) Each method works equally quickly

The correct answer is A:) Through an IV.

148) The enzymes in the liver:

    A) Are normally active
    B) Metabolize naturally occurring chemicals in the body
    C) Are specialized to deal with foreign chemicals
    D) Are not different than other enzymes in the body

The correct answer is C:) Are specialized to deal with foreign chemicals. The enzymes in the liver are different than other enzymes throughout the body as they are normally inactive until a foreign substance is introduced to the body.

149) Toulene is

    A) A lipid
    B) A stimulant
    C) Water soluable
    D) None of the above

The correct answer is C:) Water soluable.

150) What does FAS stand for?

    A) Fetal Alcohol Sickness
    B) Fetal Addiction Syndrome
    C) Fetal Alcohol Syndrome
    D) Fetal Addiction Sickness

The correct answer is C:) Fetal Alcohol Syndrome.

151) Which of the following is a stimulant?

    A) Cocaine
    B) Beer
    C) Wine
    D) Cannabis

The correct answer is A:) Cocaine. Cocaine is a stimulant.

152) Which of the following would NOT be considered synesthesia?

    A) Tasting a sound
    B) Hearing a thought
    C) Feeling a sight
    D) Seeing a sound

The correct answer is B:) Hearing a thought. Synesthesia is a mixing of senses. Thinking is not a sense, so hearing a thought is not an example of synesthesia.

153) Which of the following categories of drugs make you see or hear things that are not there?

A) Stimulants
B) Depressants
C) Hallucinogens
D) None of the above

The correct answer is C:) Hallucinogens. Hallucinogens make your body experience sensations that are not real.

154) MDMA (Ecstasy), GHB, Rohypnol (Ruffies), Clarity, and Ketamine (Special K) area all examples of what kinds of drugs?

A) Depressants
B) Club drugs
C) Uppers
D) Prescription drugs

The correct answer is B:) Club drugs. Most of these drugs are colorless, flavorless, and odorless. These can be dangerous to non-users as they can be added to beverages undetected.

155) Which of the following are narcotics?

A) Peyote
B) Codeine
C) LSD
D) Advil

The correct answer is B:) Codeine. Codeine is a narcotic, which is any drug derived from opium.

156) Which of the following is the correct abbreviation for carboxyhemoglobin?

A) COHb
B) CBHn
C) CHGo
D) CbxG

The correct answer is A:) COHb. Carboxyhemoglobin is the term for the combination of carbon monoxide with oxygen carrying hemoglobin.

157) Which of the following is NOT a withdrawal symptom of cocaine?

A) Irritability
B) Depression
C) Vomiting and shaking
D) Craving

The correct answer is C:) Vomiting and shaking. Cocaine has few visible withdrawal symptoms. However, the symptoms it does have (such as irritability, depression, and intense craving) are severe.

158) A sedative drug will

A) Decrease heart rate
B) Increase heart rate
C) Improve eye sight
D) Increase endorphins

The correct answer is A:) Decrease heart rate. Sedatives produce a relaxing effect, but not sleep.

159) Which of the following is an amphetamine?

A) Caffeine
B) Advil
C) Wine
D) LSD

The correct answer is A:) Caffeine. Caffeine is an amphetamine. It is a stimulant to the central nervous system.

160) Which of the following is a common gateway drug?

A) Steroids
B) Crack
C) LSD
D) Marijuana

The correct answer is D:) Marijuana. Marijuana is considered a gateway drug. The more you use it, the more likely you are to become addicted to more and more powerful drugs.

161) Which of the following is NOT considered a possible fetal alcohol syndrome disorder?

A) Poor coordination
B) Learning disabilities
C) Hyperactive behavior
D) Liver failure

The correct answer is D:) Liver failure. Poor coordination, learning disabilities, and hyperactive behavior are all possible FAS characteristics.

162) Which of the following is illegal to individuals 16 years of age?

A) Alcohol
B) Tobacco
C) Chew
D) All of the above

The correct answer is D:) All of the above. Although some states differ on the age you must be to purchase tobacco, none of them allow it to be purchased at 16. You must be 21 to purchase alcohol in every state in the U.S.

163) Which of the following is a withdrawal symptom for Marijuana?

A) Anger
B) Chills
C) Insomnia
D) All of the above

The correct answer is D:) All of the above. The withdrawal symptoms for Marijuana are many and include: anger, irritibility, depression, restlessness, weight loss, anxiety, insomnia, nervousness, headache, stomach ache, increased sweating, fever, chills and shakiness.

164) Which act taxed the importation and sale of opiates?

    A) The 1914 Harrison Act
    B) The 1938 Food, Drug, and Cosmetic Act
    C) The 1962 Kefauver-Harris amendments
    D) The 1906 Pure Food and Drugs Act

The correct answer is A:) The 1914 Harrison Act. The purpose of the Harrison Act was to "provide for the registration of, with collectors of internal revenue, and to impose a special tax on all persons who produce, import, manufacture, compound, deal in, dispense, sell, distribute, or give away opium or coca leaves, their salts, derivatives, or preparations, and for other purposes."

165) Which of the following drugs is approved by the FDA to treat insomnia?

    A) Xanax
    B) Lunesta
    C) Claratin
    D) Mescaline

The correct answer is B:) Lunesta. Lunesta is approved by the FDA to treat insomnia.

166) Which of the following chemicals is used as an inhalant?

    A) Toluene
    B) Codeine
    C) Telazol
    D) MDMA

The correct answer is A:) Toluene. Toluene is a general solvent, a chemical in many paint thinners and sealants. It is an ingredient in many products like glue and additives to gasoline and jet fuel. Sniffing highly concentrated amounts of the chemicals such as toluene, in solvents or aerosol sprays can directly induce heart failure and death.

167) How many major arteries supply the brain with blood?

    A) Three
    B) Four
    C) Five
    D) Six

The correct answer is B:) Four. The brain has four major arteries that supply it with blood.

168) St. John's Wort is used to treat which of the following?

    A) Insomnia
    B) Fatigue
    C) Depression
    D) None of the above

The correct answer is C:) Depression. St. John's Wort is used as an over the counter remedy for mild depression.

169) Kava kava is used to treat which of the following?

    A) Insomnia
    B) Fatigue
    C) Depression
    D) None of the above

The correct answer is A:) Insomnia.

170) Cocaine is included in which schedule of drugs?

    A) Schedule I
    B) Schedule II
    C) Schedule III
    D) Schedule IV

The correct answer is B:) Schedule II.

171) What is the most common way for new drugs to be discovered?

    A) Clinical study of current drugs
    B) Synthesizing new compounds
    C) Accidental observation of effects
    D) Scientific hypotheses

The correct answer is C:) Accidental observation of effects. Most new drugs are discovered accidentally when certain results were not searched for.

172) Which of the following is NOT a withdrawal symptom of heroin?

    A) Aches
    B) Nausea
    C) Muscle cramps
    D) Heroin has no known withdrawal symptoms

The correct answer is D:) Heroin has no known withdrawal symptoms. Aches, nausea, and muscle cramps are all examples of heroin's many severe withdrawal symptoms.

173) Xanax, Darvocet and Ambien are considered to be on which Schedule?

    A) Schedule II
    B) Schedule III
    C) Schedule IV
    D) Schedule V

The correct answer is C:) Schedule IV. These drugs are considered to have low potential for abuse and low risk of dependence.

174) What is the term to describe the interaction between two or more drugs where the effects of the drugs combined are greater than the addition of the effects of the drugs taken separately?

    A) Summation
    B) Antagonism
    C) Mitigation
    D) Potentiation

The correct answer is D:) Potentiation. Potentiation is the term used to describe the result of the interaction of two or more drugs where the end effect is greater than the sum of the effects of the drugs taken separately.

175) Inhaling from a inhalant-soaked rag is called

    A) Bagging
    B) Huffing
    C) Sniffing
    D) Snorting

The correct answer is B:) Huffing.

176) The branch of pharmacology concerned with the movement of drugs within the body is called

    A) Dose response curve
    B) Pharmacokinetics
    C) Potentiation
    D) Pharmacy study

The correct answer is B:) Pharmacokinetics.

Test Taking Strategies

Here are some test-taking strategies that are specific to this test and to other DSST tests in general:

- Keep your eyes on the time. Pay attention to how much time you have left.

- Read the entire question and read all the answers. Many questions are not as hard to answer as they may seem. Sometimes, a difficult sounding question really only is asking you how to read an accompanying chart. Chart and graph questions are on most DANTES/DSST tests and should be an easy free point.

- If you don't know the answer immediately, the new computer-based testing lets you mark questions and come back to them later if you have time.

- Read the wording carefully. Some words can give you hints to the right answer. There are no exceptions to an answer when there are words in the question such as always, all or none. If one of the answer choices includes most or some of the right answers, but not all, then that is not the answer. Here is an example:

> The primary colors include all of the following:
>
> A) Red, Yellow, Blue, Green
>
> B) Red, Green, Yellow
>
> C) Red, Orange, Yellow
>
> D) Red, Yellow, Blue

Although item A includes all the right answers, it also includes an incorrect answer, making it incorrect. If you didn't read it carefully, were in a hurry, or didn't know the material well, you might fall for this.

- Make a guess on a question that you do not know the answer to. There is no penalty for an incorrect answer. Eliminate the answer choices that you know are incorrect. For example, this will let your guess be a 1 in 3 chance instead.

Test Preparation

How much you need to study depends on your knowledge of a subject area. If you are interested in literature, took it in school, or enjoy reading then your study and preparation for the literature or humanities test will not need to be as intensive as that of someone who is new to literature.

This book is much different than the regular DANTES study guides. This book actually teaches you the information that you need to know to pass the test. If you are particularly interested in an area, or feel that you want more information, do a quick search online. We've tried not to include too much depth in areas that are not as essential on the test. Everything in this book will be on the test. It is important to understand all major theories and concepts listed in the table of contents. It is also important to know any bolded words.

Don't worry if you do not understand or know a lot about the area. With minimal study, you can complete and pass the test.

One of the fallacies of other test books is test questions. People assume that the **content** of the questions are similar to what will be on the test. **That is not the case.** They are only there to test your "test taking skills" so for those who know to read a question carefully, there is not much added value from taking a "fake" test. If you did not score high on this sample test, do not be alarmed. We use sample test questions to teach you new information in a condensed way.

To prepare for the test, make a series of goals. Allot a certain amount of time to review the information you have already studied and to learn additional material. Take notes as you study; it will help you learn the material.

 *Legal Note*

FLASHCARDS

This section contains flashcards for you to use to further your understanding of the material and test yourself on important concepts, names or dates. Read the term or question then flip the page over to check the answer on the back. Keep in mind that this information may not be covered in the text of the study guide. Take your time to study the flashcards, you will need to know and understand these concepts to pass the test.

The First Pharmalogical Revolution

Hashish is what type of drug?

Which Act created drug scheduling?

Alcohol is what type of drug?

Heroin is in what drug schedule?

Which two federal agencies determine what schedule a drug is classified as?

The fourth pharmalogical revolution

Alcoholic hepatitis

Cannabis

Ace The *Clep*

Vaccines

Ace The *Clep*

Depressant

Ace The *Clep*

CSA

Ace The *Clep*

DEA and FDA

Ace The *Clep*

Schedule I

Ace The *Clep*

Inflammation in the liver

Ace The *Clep*

"the pill"

Ace The *Clep*

Codeine is what type of drug?

What are the properties of a Schedule I drug?

Ritalin is why type of drug?

Marijuana is in what drug schedule?

Morphine is what type of drug?

Potentiation

Peyote is what kind of drug?

Proof

Highly addictive, and has no
accepted medical purpose

Narcotic

Schedule I

Stimulant

The result when two drugs
combine and the resulting
effects are greater than
the effects of the two drugs
added together

Narcotic

The alcohol percentage in the
beverage

Hallucinogen

BAC

PCP is what type of drug?

What is the most commonly used illegal drug?

Opium is created from what plant?

Anabolic steroids

Korsakoff's syndrome symptoms

Examples of depressants

Bong

Hallucinogen

Blood alcohol content

Poppy

Marijuana

Amnesia

Increase muscle mass, protein synthesis, and bone density

A way marijuana is smoked

Alcohol, Barbiturates, Xanax

Confabulation

Narcan

Benzodiazepines is what type of drug?

Valium is used as a

Cocaine is what type of drug?

What is used to treat anxiety disorders?

Benzodiazepines include

Ecstasy is what type of drug?

Used to counter the effects of
opiate overdose

When a person "creates"
memories and believes them
to be real

relaxant

Depressant

Xanax

Stimulant

Hallucinogen

Valium, Xanax, and Ativan

Psychoactive drugs effect what?

Peyote is what kind of plant?

LD50/ED50

Methadone is what type of drug?

Marijuana is made from what plant?

The Second Pharmalogical Revolution

Drugs which depress a person's system are called

Thalidomide

Cactus

The brain

Narcotic

The ED50 value is the
"Effective Dose" for 50% of
the population, or the average
effective dose. The LD50
value is the "Lethal Dose" for
50% of the population.

Antibiotics

Cannabis

Originally prescribed for
morning sickness, recalled
for birth defects of deformed
limbs

Barbiturates

Examples of stimulants

DSM-IV

Example of synesthesia

Opium is what type of drug?

Stages of detoxification

Examples of routes to administer drugs through mucous membranes

What does elevated hepatic enzymes levels indicate?

Another name for stimulants

Diagnostic and Statistical
Manual of Mental Disorders

Cocaine, amphetamines

Narcotic

Smelling colors

Inhalation, under the tongue,
snorting or sniffing through
nose

Cleansing, removal of cells
killed by toxins, rebuilding
tissues

Uppers

Liver damage because of
drug use

Narcotic is Greek for what?

What is the fastest way to take a drug?

What drug is known as the date rape drug?

ADHD is an acronym for

LSD is what type of drug?

What are the withdrawal symptoms of heroin?

CSA stands for

What are the withdrawal symptoms of LSD?

Through an IV

Stupor

Attention deficit hyperactivity
disorder

Rohypnol or Flunitrazepam

Aches, nausea, and muscle
cramps

Hallucinogen

No known withdrawal
symptoms

Controlled Substances Act

Examples of narcotics

What are the withdrawal symptoms of PCP?

FAS

Examples of hallucinogens

Cocaine is created from what plant?

What drug is given to recovering heroin addicts to curb their withdrawal?

Barbiturates are what type of drug?

What is the street name for cannabis?

Violence, muscle rigidity,
coma, and convulsions

Opium, morphine, codeine,
heroin, methadone

Ecstasy, LSD, Acid,
Mescaline

Fetal Alcohol Syndrome

Methadone

Coca plant

Marijuana

Depressant

Made in the USA
San Bernardino, CA
24 January 2018